What Millionaires, Best-selling Authors, and One Reverend Are Saying:

"I am your biggest fan and promoter. I love that people get to hear your turned-on message!"

— **Mark V. Hansen**
Co-author, *Chicken Soup for the Soul*

"This is a book you gotta read! I loved the way it gets in ~~y~~ one. Just like Wendy, this book is electric. It's mind-expanding and playful and bright and full of life. You're gonna love this book. It has Wendy Power...you'll find out just what that means when you read it. Get it."

— **Robert G. Allen**
Best-selling author, *Multiple Streams of Income, The One Minute Millionaire* and *Cash in a Flash: Fast Money in Slow Times*

"Why Marry a Millionaire? Just Be One! shows you how to become financially free, balanced, passionate, and live a powerful life. If you want to make a dramatic difference in your life now, read this book!"

— **T. Harv Eker**
Best-selling author, *Secrets of the Millionaire Mind*

"Wendy's can-do attitude is a breath of fresh air in today's frenzied world of business. Her tips are easy to adapt and make becoming a millionaire seem utterly attainable! Wendy's gift isn't merely her incredible expertise on how-to, it's her amazing ability to transform women's self-image that truly makes her a superstar!!! And in a perfect world, our 'Wonder-Woman Wendy' would definitely make house calls!!"

— **Stacey Schieffelin**
President, ybf (your best friend)
14-year success record in direct sales on HSN (Home Shopping Network) with cosmetic and apparel sales in excess of $150 million

"Where Wendy Robbins leads, I will follow!"

— **Byron Katie**
Best-selling author, *Love What Is, I Need Your Love — Is That True?*

"Wendy Robbins is a rare blend of journalist and visionary. She makes time to know her material. She asks the right questions, in just the right way, to guide us into the hidden wisdom of our lives."

— **Gregg Braden**
Best-selling author, *The God Code, The Divine Matrix,* and *The Spontaneous Healing of Belief*

"Wendy Robbins has an infectious enthusiasm. With profound generosity, she has gifted us with a practical guide to knock out our 'old stories' about wealth and happiness and replace them with confidence to follow our 'new story' and dream."
— **Justine Willis Toms**
Co-founder, New Dimensions Media/Radio
Author, *Small Pleasures: Finding Grace in a Chaotic World*

"During this age of accelerated change, overwhelming complexity, and tremendous competition, this book empowers women to not only learn how to create massive wealth but also how to leverage their knowledge and skills to make a difference on the planet. Wendy's book is needed now more than ever before. Fortunately, she is the message that she brings. She has grown through and overcome, therefore she speaks from a place of knowing."
— **Les Brown**
Named in Top 5 Speakers in the World by Toastmasters International
Author, *Live Your Dreams*

"Wendy Robbins is the perfect person to show you how to design and actualize a life you are passionate about — and make a lot of money doing it. If you're ready to take charge of your life and be the person you've been waiting for, Wendy will show you how! Buckle your seat belts and get ready for a magical ride!"
— **Cynthia Kersey**
Best-selling author, *Unstoppable* and *Unstoppable Women*

"Wendy does her homework, asks profound questions and has a great sense of humor."
— **Barbara Marx Hubbard**
President, Foundation for Conscious Evolution, and leader on the growing edge of the women's movement

"Wendy Robbins gives voice to cutting-edge thinking and is a visionary — always making the information clear, easy to understand, and astounding."
— **Lynn Andrews**
Best-selling author, *Jaguar Woman*

"Wendy is one of the most innovative and inspiring individuals I have ever met! Her desire and drive to help other people and to have success in life is amazing. Wendy is pure entrepreneurial talent."
— **Randy Garn**
Co-founder, Prosper, Inc.

"Wendy's style is loving and respectful and promotes the journey of personal healing and growth. We need the Wendy Robbinses of the world to step forth. I hope she can find a platform to reach millions, to magnify and promote healing."
— **Reverend Ted Wiard LPCC, CGC**

Published by
Nowhere To Millionaire™ LLC
Taos, New Mexico

Personalized e-book available, customized with your or your company's name!
To get it and other continuing education products, or for large sales, visit
www.nowheretomillionaire.com or e-mail **workwithwendy@gmail.com**.

Distributed by Hay House, Inc.
www.hayhouse.com®

Contact author:
www.nowheretomillionaire.com

www.askwendynow.com
(free training, ask Wendy your burning questions)

www.facebook.com/wendyrobbins

www.twitter.com/wendyrobbins

www.tingletribe.com
(community mastermind group)

www.whymarryamillionairejustbeone.com

13 12 11 10   4 3 2 1
1st edition, November 2010

Printed in the United States of America

CONTENTS

"Greed is not good."
— **Wendy Robbins**

"To thine own self be true."
— **William Shakespeare**

To paraphrase Clarissa Pinkola Estes:
"If you have ever been called defiant, incorrigible, unruly, or rebellious, you are on the right track."

"Create the wow of now, a daily legacy, live, love, fully and ecstatically!"
— **Wendy Robbins**

INTRODUCTION: Hello, You Gorgeous Star!

Are you ready for a mind-blowing, heart-opening, life-changing, triple-shot of espresso for the millionaire's soul?

Let's start with a couple of questions.

What do you think you need to do this year to double your money, business, happiness, and time off?

What strategies have you already tried that did or didn't work for you?

I've posed these questions to hundreds of people, so I can probably guess your answers. You worry over a lack of money, balance, knowledge, and purpose. You want to know that you matter, make a difference, and have time to do what you love. You want to make more cash so you can stop working, you want to know you and your family are taken care of, and you want to have fun, right?

You know that if you addressed certain aspects of your life, you would have a better idea of what you really want to do when you grow up. You know there are ways to double your money and/or your business. The challenge is that you haven't figured them out. You've tried stuff that didn't work the way you thought it would — some have brought results, but not nearly enough, right?

I get it. The good news is, I have the solutions for you *now*. What is in this book has helped a lot of people with very similar challenges. The results have been amazing!

If your real ambition is to succeed, you need to follow a simple framework — a system — before it can happen for you. If you are deciding whether this book is right for you, hesitate no longer! *Get it now* — because the value is life-changing. *There is no time to waste!*

This book is organized in a way that is logical, easy-to-follow, and inspiring. The first half shows you how to create, maintain, and grow your millionaire mind-set; how to find your purpose and create a legacy every day. The second half contains practical, step-by-step blueprints that demonstrate how to create the money by reinventing yourself, outsourcing, sharing your dreams with investors/buyers, and working with others so you can focus and have time to do what you love. Sound toe-curling?

There are many books out there promising you the secret to instant wealth and eternal happiness. This isn't one of those books.

This is a "question the status quo" system, an interactive coaching dialogue that challenges you to journal, face, and answer intimate and provocative questions. You will learn how to connect with other like-minded people, break through your barriers, reevaluate stale influences of the past, upload new belief systems, and take continuous action — the culmination of which will lead you to ecstatic and meaningful success.

It is not the secret, it is the answer to the secrets of success.

Your mission possible, should you choose to accept it, is to dramatically change your life in 72 hours. Are you up for the challenge? The clock is ticking, starting now!

So, who am I? Who is this Wendy Robbins?

I am your mirror. I am your results-oriented coach, and I hold the treasure map you have been dreaming of.

My basic story goes like this: I went from having $10,000 in credit-card debt to making millions. My partner and I did it in just a few years. A lot of mistakes were made — errors I am going to help you avoid — like being stressed out, unbalanced, unfocused, out of control, and angry. I spent a lot of time blaming others, not having fun, and sabotaging myself.

I thought money would solve all my problems. Have you thought that, too? I realize now, overall, the money didn't make me feel happier, safer, or more in control. Feeding the cycle of consumerism is seductive. *More! Faster! Bigger! Sexier!* It seems so intriguing...so you run out and get the toys, then realize that altruism is so much more exhilarating. Money can be euphoric — it can change your world and help you change other people's worlds — which is why I want to show you how to create real wealth that you can pay forward.

I don't subscribe to the notion that "greed is good," nor do I believe in taking advantage of people and justifying it by saying, "It's just business." I'm not interested in working 80-hour weeks — or even 40-hour weeks — and missing out on precious time doing what I love. I want you to enjoy this journey.

I am interested in money with a soul, in enriching your essence, your core, your reason for being alive.

I'm focused on conscious business, creating a legacy a day, being green, spirituality, recession-proofing your life, being in service to others; and working where you want, when you want, with whomever you want.

Many business or money-making books ask you to be someone you really aren't. They tell you you'll be happy if you make a lot of cash. If you aren't happy with what you have now, will *more* make you happier?

I want you to be YOU.

As a child, were you told to find someone who would "take care of you financially"? Did you think that the only way to nirvana was to marry a millionaire? Here's what I say to that (minus a few four-letter words):

WHY MARRY A MILLIONAIRE? JUST BE ONE!!

Are you still there on your fluffy chaise lounge waiting for your prince to come rescue you? What? He's late? Well, that's okay...he probably just took a wrong turn. So what do you do? You call your girlfriend, who assures you that he's definitely on his way but is just too stubborn to ask for directions.

Quit waiting for someone else to make the money for you. Stop working for your money and let your money work for you!

Own your power! You have permission to be rich! You can have a blast being wealthy — as you! It's not about the money; it's about how you get there and how true you are to yourself and others in the process. **Be rich and be *you* as well.**

You've heard of the Horse Whisperer and the Dog Whisperer, right?

I am the Authenticity Whi$perer. Give me 72 hours and I will radically and richly change your life for the better. Guaranteed! Think of this experience as a long-term love story with you, your soul's life purpose, and the heart of money. I'm the matchmaker.

I love gifts, don't you? Give me a sale, a discount, something for free, a party, anything in silk or velvet, and you'll have my attention.

Your gift is a free coaching session. All you need to do to claim the gift is read this book and take action. You don't get it until we're through, though, because you're not ready for it yet. Trust me!

Together we're going to change our life game. The main rule is *play to win*.

You are the source as well as the participant. You're not the critic and you're not a fan in the bleachers. You're certainly not a wallflower — in fact, those people will be escorted out by security.

How you do anything is how you do everything!

You will be held accountable for your actions. You may as well memorize this sentence now: "If it's to be, it's up to me."

I'll always ask you to be authentic. Most people are not genuine or sincere. What does that mean? It means that a lot of us are pretending, doing things that we don't believe in, living a short life filled with stress and devoid of intimate connections. I'd hazard a guess and say the majority of human beings think life is meaningless and struggle daily to find its purpose.

I have worked with many of these people. They feel stagnant, unfocused, and unbalanced. They are not doing what they like to do. Life has become a big-time, serious bore.

Sound familiar? You've likely said, "I can't do this anymore! I need something different in my life!" Or how about this: "My life sucks! How did I end up here?"

My grandmother always said, "Oy vey, if I had a nickel for every time I've heard that...." That's how I feel. Nearly every person I've worked with has thrown their own pity party. I have, too.

I said to them what I'm going to say to you now: *Wake up! Quit living your life with glazed eyes, going through the automated motions of your day, your week, your life. You were put here to do amazing things for yourself and for the world!*

It's time to stop making excuses. Start creating the life of your dreams!

You can do anything you want.

Dream of being a millionaire? It's possible. Want to travel the world and explore exotic places? Why not? Yearn to live a rich life without sacrificing your soul? You can do that.

But don't start clearing out your cubicle yet, because we have some work to do before you break out the cardboard boxes.

You can meet anyone you want, travel anywhere for little to no cost, appear on your favorite talk shows, live in a mansion, change the world. Interested? That's what this awe-inspiring, goose-bumpy, tingly adventure is all about!

Are you waiting until you are "ready to retire" to retire?

Why? No, seriously...why? What excuses do you continue to believe? "I can't do _____ until I have enough _____." "My past is so bad. I have a lot of tragic stories and that's why I can't _____."

Why are you fighting for your limiting beliefs? Why defend being broke or unhappy? It's time to consciously design your new "wow" of a life.

In the 2007 movie *The Bucket List,* Jack Nicholson's and Morgan Freeman's characters create a "to do" list of all the things they still want to do after each is given less than a year to live. The two men go on to fulfill every single item on their lists.

Could you do that? Sure you could! But first, you have to create the list.

What makes you so excited, so energized, so touched and motivated that you have to do it before you die? Sit down and make a long list — then go out and complete every item on it. Do at least two things on the list within 72 hours.

Excuses are neither accepted nor tolerated. Start writing five things now.

1. _____

2. _____

3. _____

4. _____

5. _____

What's on your list? Travel? Fame? Fortune? Love? Change the world? Create a legacy? Forgive someone? Love yourself and really *get* that you are worthy, lovable, and deserving of great things?

How many of these possibilities can you relate to?

You've taken the first step toward fulfilling your destiny by embarking on this fast-paced trip with me. You'll learn how to:

- Be real and not care what others think of you
- Give yourself permission to be rich
- Outsource your work and your life
- Make investors and buyers beg to invest in your dreams
- Sell products in 24 hours — even if you don't have any!
- Make money online without knowing what you are doing
- Sell houses without owning them
- Make 20 percent on your money with little to no risk
- Work from home — or anywhere you want!
- Run a virtual store from your hammock
- Do business like Tom Sawyer (hire ten people to make you $50 profit an hour, 40 hours a week, and make $1 million in 10 months!)
- Live like a millionaire now — even if you are broke!

CHAPTER 1: Say What?!?!

You can make back the money you paid for this book in just 24 hours.

SAY WHAT?!?!

Before you read any further, I want you to *bake cupcakes and sell them*.

Wait a second, did I really just ask you to conduct your own bake sale? Isn't this book about being a millionaire? Yep, it sure is...and here's how cupcakes can make you millions:

Cordia Harrington is a former investment banker who loved to bake. Cupcakes were her passion, whisked from her own series of recipes.

She took those mouth-watering masterpieces and opened her own store. Within hours she had sold out of her first huge batch. Soon she was selling thousands a day to people forming lines that wrapped around the block!

What is Cordia doing today? She's been featured on *Oprah, Good Morning America*, and *The Today Show* and is selling her baked bits of heaven to customers around the world.

Cupcakes, anyone?

My friend Tim grew up in a poor, non-English-speaking family. He believed in the dream and became a multimillionaire before he turned 30. He loves money and taught his kids to appreciate it, too.

His son earns money to buy extra toys, raises money for homeless people, and takes toys to kids at hospitals. His goal is to make a million by the time he is 12.

The boy was eating a slice of birthday cake on his fifth birthday when he turned to his dad and said, "Daddy, I want to make money. I'm gonna bake cupcakes. Can I get a loan from you to start my business? I'll pay you back with interest, and I promise to keep my room clean!"

Pretty irresistible offer, right? Thus began his business, and when I met him he was onstage with his dad, screaming and waving his hands wildly. "Buy my cupcakes. My cupcakes gooooood!!! Better ruuuuunnnn they go fast!" Sure enough, a hundred adults ran tripping over each other to get their sugar fix. In just three minutes and 22 seconds, he'd made $200! He said, "Dad, I like making money. It's really cool!"

Then he had another great idea: why not Franchise his business model, showing other kids how to run their own baked-goods business? He was paid a small licensing fee to show them exactly what to do.

I asked him about having a lemonade stand. "I tried it, but it's too tough and competitive. There's not enough profit based on how much work it is. I'd rather make money easily and have time to play with my friends."

He's five...what's your excuse?!

This proves that mastering the millionaire mind-set can start at any age!

I once appeared on the *Montel Williams Show* with a woman who grew up poor and undereducated, the daughter of immigrant farm workers who had created a fabulous recipe for salsa. She saw an opportunity and went for it — and now makes millions in retail sales. *¿Bueno, sí?*

Another guest on the same episode was a bedridden woman with a serious addiction to romance novels. She complained that many of the bestsellers involved stories that were unrealistic and far-fetched. How did she solve this problem? She wrote her own! She discovered that she could complete two books a week. She soon developed a huge fan base and a multimillion-dollar business. So if you are currently looking at your lover affectionately as "Plan B," romance novels may be the way to go!

What's the moral of these stories? If they can do it, you can, too! You need to take action now, today. Action leads to results — no action then no, nada, nyet results, right? If you get discouraged, remember these encouraging words that I got from a napkin: "It is happy hour somewhere." And like Dr. Seuss said,

"Funny things are everywhere." Remember to laugh a lot as you discover your own way to make $3,000 a day.

I'm going to ask you to do things you may initially resist, tell you things about yourself you may deny. I will love you, perhaps, like you've never been loved. I see your potential in ways that you may not be able to see right now. Think of this journey we are about to take as a *Thelma and Louise* road trip — without killing anyone or driving over a cliff.

What I ask in return is that you remain true to your desires and consciously redesign every aspect of your life. Remember that this requires discipline. Do you have what it takes?

WARNING: This book may not work for you if you are only one TV dinner away from a nervous breakdown.

Be honest — you might be just a tad on the lazy side, right? Does the highlight of your life involve watching every reality show on TV? We need to change that.

It's time to star in your own reality show.

It requires attention and a commitment from you. You have to want to change — and you have to want it more than your lazy and fearful self doesn't want to. It's that easy. And that hard.

I'll give you an example of how I overcame my fears and grew to trust my inner Xena.

Someone once handed me a thick, wooden board and told me to break it in half with my hand. I thought the guy was out of his testosterone-driven mind. All I could think was how I knew I was going to break something, and the smart money was on my *hand,* not the board.

I automatically approached the feat with fear. Not exactly the best strategy.

So I tried a new approach. I visualized breaking the board, no matter what. Nothing was going to stop me. I looked at the board, concentrated on it and beyond it. I saw it break in my mind...and I went for it with pure, wild abandon.

What do you think happened? Was the emergency room my next destination? Not exactly.

That thick piece of wood broke in half effortlessly. My hand was fine. My worry was gone. I had summoned my courage and knew I could and would do anything I wanted.

That is the lesson I want you to learn. Your board is your doubt, your excuses, your uncertainties. You are going to smash them all. Break it right in half, courageously and easily. When you feel your fears taking over, think of the board. Imagine yourself breaking through, completely obliterating whatever it is that is standing in your way.

Allow your passion to move you forward.

Look your excuses in the face and tell them, "You're not the boss of me!" then take a step back and understand *why* you have allowed them to be up to this point.

Speaking of WHY, consider the uses of adversity. Something is stopping you from acting on your dreams, right? We'll identify it and then we'll change it so you act, creating results. Figure out WHY you want what you think you want.

Imagine if I asked you to make $5,000 in the next 72 hours.

Sounds a lot like the wood slab that guy gave me to break. It seems scary and impossible. Your excuses may be shouting at you and you are ready to shut the book with a bunch of "I can't..." stories, right?

What if I said that someone you love needed an operation, didn't have insurance, and you only had 72 hours to raise $5,000 or they would die?

You would find a way to get that money, wouldn't you? You would be creative and courageous, with no excuses or obstacles to stop you, right?

So what is your WHY? Make up a powerful, back-against-the-wall, life-or-death decision and know that nothing will stop you. You will change radically in 72 hours with your big WHY guiding you and your actions. Write it down here:

My big WHY to be financially free is _____

_____

_____

Whatever that WHY might be, it must resonate with you emotionally. You need to be so passionate and so driven to accomplish your goals that nothing can or will get in your way. Got it? Good.

Remember, I am not giving you the tools to pursue a fad diet. This is not a get-rich-quick scheme, producing immediate results that will disappear after a week or a month. The gift I am giving you can — and will — change your life forever if you let it. It may take you one, three, five, or ten years to become a millionaire. You must change your thoughts, beliefs, feelings, and habits so that you start living richly in the millionaire mind-set, thereby honestly changing your life one thought at a time.

It is crucial that you accept that who you are **now** is amazing.

You are not lacking anything. You are not wrong or bad. You are simply open to receiving more. You have a reason for wanting new qualities, new things, new goals, new tales, or new emptiness and stillness.

Many people read books like this one and begin to feel miserable, as if they are not living up to the person the book is asking them to be or explore. Obsessive thoughts take over and tell you that you have no right to be rich. They say, "You can't be a millionaire, are you kidding me? Ha!" When you spend money, your thoughts remind you, "Oooops! I spent the grocery money on purses again, so much for being a millionaire!"

Understand one thing right now: your story, as it is told this very moment, is one of sorrow, happiness, weakness, power, selfishness, generosity, lack, and abundance. You are a paradox, a bit manic if you are attached to only one story or emotion. These are merely filters you have been using that allow you to prove your point and be right. Is that working? Really? Is it?

Your life is the story you make up, create, and tell.

So far, you've made up stories that put you in a headlock. Or maybe it's a heartlock. Perhaps a hurtlock? What about a gridlock? That doesn't sound like a very happy tale to me, certainly not one I'd want to kick back and read on a beach-side lounge chair. It is one of endless suffering, misery, and wanting what you don't have.

The yawns, I mean, the yarns about your past — presently making you feel weak or believe that life is unfair — offer many lessons.

Grieve fully over painful situations and then let them go. Get the deeper meaning.

If you have been ill, recognize this time as a healing opportunity, a chance to know that *you* are not your *body*. Learn how to ride the wave of the pain — rest, nurture yourself, learn to love your flexibility and your strength, exercise, focus on your healing and optimal health because focusing on the pain or spending time obsessing about when you were younger won't help you heal. Get it?

Which do you value more, health or disease? You will know, based on your actions, which leads to results. If you eat processed foods, are a couch potato, smoke and drink, you don't value your health, do you?

Behind the actions are thoughts and feelings and beliefs you've made up about your self-worth. I simply ask that you choose to value your life, your health, your self-esteem more than being sick, overweight, or lazy, letting your unhealthy habits run your life.

It takes effort to change, and you are worth it!

If you made a lot of money and lost it due to bad financial choices, grieve, learn the lessons, see the gifts in the challenge, and make better choices. Perhaps you will learn not to equate your personal worth with the size of your bank accounts.

If you are broke or regularly say, "I'm poor," then you value not having enough, not feeling like you deserve more — or you feel you are not capable of making money. You get to explore your beliefs, change your actions, and watch your results change. Value yourself, your time in exchange for money, and you will become wealthy by taking constant action, tweaking what does and doesn't work based on your results.

Learn to stop asking for success and preparing for failure; you will get the situation you prepare for.

If you have just broken up with your partner, grieve fully, learn the lessons, and move on. Perhaps this time you will finally learn to value yourself. You'll see the importance of taking yourself on dates, loving yourself the way you want another to love you, being more choosy next time, and opening your heart even more. You'll notice how the pain tenderized your heart so you become more compassionate and can one day thank your ex.

It's up to you to find meaning in what appears to be an unhappy story, event, ,or circumstance. Some will wallow in pain all their lives, becoming defeated, despondent, depressed, and discouraged. Others use the hurt as a catalyst to being powerful. They value being fully alive, make international policy changes, or run a first marathon in spite of being arthritic and 60.

Why do some people primarily live their past melancholy stories and others don't? Same situation or circumstance and two different ways to respond to death, betrayal, loss, and grief — how is this possible? The *meaning* that is derived from the story is what makes all the difference.

Let's explore the same situation and two different responses. One individual sees a painful situation as a learning experience. This person derives meaning from the hurt, grows from the challenges, and learns how to respond the next time. The other individual holds on to pain or pretends that it doesn't affect him or her. As a result, there is a feeling of regret, resignation, cynicism, doubt, fear, hurt, grief, numbness or guilt. We all know people like this — or perhaps *we* resemble this description.

At this point in our lives, we may even defend why we are who we've become. We may get angry with someone or argue for our limitations because we've become an entitled victim. Anyone who can't see why we are poor, heartbroken, and apathetic is insensitive and unworthy of our friendship. We need people who will feed our story, our belief, our inaction. We need people who will let us drink, do drugs, complain, smoke, get fat or sick, and lose our inner light. We don't want people to participate powerfully in our lives. We've given up and are addicted to only one possibility, even though the opposite is equally true and equally possible. Maybe friends sometimes don't call us on our stuff because misery loves company. Did you ever think of that?

I am not that friend. There is a good chance that you may not like everything I say because I will ask you to value yourself to spite your pain, to challenge everything you feel, think, and believe.

If you are obsessed by your story, you'll be challenged!

It's difficult at times to remember your options when you are wallowing in the hurt, sting, or wound — it is addictive. This is why I am here to stop you from suffering when you can do what Byron Katie says: "Love what is."

If you don't, you will suffer. Why embrace struggle?

This may seem like an impossible task now, and that's okay. Just stay open, please, because we have a lot of shifts like that to try out if we are going to radically change our lives in 72 hours, right?

Starting now, you are going to be the conscious rather than unconscious author of your life story. You are going to be awake, aware, and heroic as you tell your tales; and from now on they are going to be extraordinary and insightful. Up until now, too many have been pitiful, boring, full of blame, and, in some cases, downright scary. That has to change, because you're really starting to freak out your audience — and not in a good way.

Your new tale starts with authenticity — that's not negotiable.

Get rid of your guilt, throw away your resentment, toss out your fear, release revenge and regret, and forget all of your doubts. Start being you — stripped to the core, starting from scratch, from a still nothingness. Hey, nothing wrong with being alive for the pure joy of it, is there? Nothing else was working, so get rid of it. Don't argue for your limitations, just do it. You'll thank me later. Worry not, I will give you specific techniques and ask you thought-provoking questions to understand how to do this.

You're about to discover the story of you, according to me.

The first tool to use is a little something I like to call **WENDY POWER**.

What is WENDY POWER?!

Here's what **WENDY POWER** means, and what it means to you:

WILDLY ENCOURAGED, NEWLY DESIGNED YOU!

Think that can be you? I know it can, within 72 hours, if you take action. Continuing to sit around on your butt hoping it happens will only get you a first-class ticket on the train to nowhere. Well, guess what? Our saga is about Nowhere to Millionaire — or Now Here to Millionaire! Hello!

Real Wealth — you can become powerful,
you can be passionate, and you will be prosperous.

I invite you to let me into your life so I can kick your butt and love you without judgment. I will help you uncover your inner sense of urgency and work with you to create results in 72 hours, guaranteed!

Ready for your first challenge? If you found out today that you only had 72 hours to live, what would you do? Think about it for a minute, then write your list here:

1. _____

2. _____

3. _____

4. _____

5. _____

You probably didn't have much trouble making your list based on your values. We all have desires, dreams, and wishes buried deep inside of us that we have been putting off. Connecting with your purpose and your passion isn't always easy — that is why making this list is the first, and most important, step.

Did you finish your list or are you stuck? If you are struggling to come up with five things you want to be, do and have before you die, look at the next page for some questions to get your juices flowing.

- Who do you need to forgive? Forgive them now.

- Who needs to hear that you love them? Tell them now.

- Is there an exotic location you've always wanted to visit? Book your trip.

- Is there a cause you believe in and you want to be part of? Join or start your own cause or movement now.

- Is your life philosophy something you can share with a million viewers on YouTube? Post it now.

- Have you always wanted to hire a PR person to make you a celebrity so people care what you have to say about changing the world? Start researching now.

- Have you made your will? Do it today.

- Have you read all of the books you want to read? Read them now.

- Want to fire your mean boss? Do it!

- Have you always dreamed of singing onstage? Go to an open mic night.

- Are you a poet and the only one who knows it? Write a stanza or two on someone's blog — or on your own — today.

- Have you complimented a stranger lately? Do it today.

- Are you too shy and want to open up more? Start today; what do you have to lose?

- Is there a book inside you waiting to get out and you just haven't let it escape yet? Record it now. You can find someone to transcribe it at **www.idictate.com**. Then offer it for sale at **www.amazon.com**.

- Is there someone you have a crush on? Tell her/him today.

- Want to write your memoir fast? Start now.

- How about starting a botanical garden? Find out how today.

- Are you inspired to speak at the United Nations? Figure out how now.

- Have you fantasized about starring in a film? Enroll in acting classes.

- Would you like to create an orphanage? Start researching how today.

- Why not have your favorite millionaire or billionaire mentor you? Contact this person today.

- Wish to get clear about your life purpose by writing out your epitaph? Do this now.

- Want to visit a cemetery so you understand what urgency is? Go today.

- Have you always wanted to pet a lion, swim with wild dolphins, kiss a whale? Book a trip now.

- Wish you could sculpt, paint, swing with kids and scream "Weeeeee!"? Get out there and do it now.

- Want to become a generous millionaire who is courageous and fully alive right now? Do it TODAY!

It doesn't matter what's on your list, it just matters that you *have* one. The more outrageous the better. Why? Because life is meant to be loving, creative, fun, expansive, and memorable. Creating your action list is the first step to manifesting your sensational dreams. The second step is taking immediate action to spite your doubts and fears.

That is WENDY POWER!

Live wildly, dynamically, enthusiastically, excitedly, playfully, confidently, gratefully, lovingly, in vivid Technicolor, ecstatically, blissfully, joyfully, steadfastly, always remembering to suck the marrow out of this day!

That is WENDY POWER in action!

Now think of someone you love unconditionally, someone who loves you and calls you on your stuff, who's supportive and sees your potential — your best friend. If you don't have one, imagine you do. Experience the loving feeling now. Expand that feeling so you are in profound gratitude.

Imagine this person calls and says, "I need an operation that costs $10,000. I'm terrified and I don't have the money. I need it in 72 hours or I'll die."

Feel that scenario as though it is real to you and ask your mind and your heart to come up with some solutions. How can you get that money if you don't have it now? What can you do to raise the money?

Get creative.

Write the ideas down now. Even if they seem to make no sense to you now, write them because you will refer to this list for inspiration to take immediate action, letting nothing stop you.

Grab a journal, your laptop, a napkin. Just start writing now. You are finding ways to be of supreme service to one person. Imagine being in selfless service to millions, to your family, to your community, or to yourself. This is what our conversation is about.

Starting today, you can begin to build your legacy.

I'm giving you 72 hours — just three days — to radically change your life and build the foundation of your legacy.

You have planned to do this for a while now, right? You have been waiting for just the right time, just the right combination of factors and life events and alignment of the stars. Well, guess what? There's no more waiting. You've been doing that for a while now — working well, is it?

If you haven't already, go back and finish your list of five things you will do before you die. Make sure to write out an expansive list on how you will make money in 72 hours to save your friend's life.

Make sure one of your five things involves joining a community site that allows you to connect with others who share your same or similar goals and ambitions. They are what you need, people who are tired of excuses and are, instead, committed to action — to finding their own **WENDY POWER**.

Sounds like a pretty good group of friends to have, doesn't it? They're not going to accept your "I was gonna, but..." or your "Oh, I plan to do that when...." They're going to kick you in the butt and motivate you to take action — and that's exactly what you need. Resistance is futile.

If you're unsure where to start, go to **www.nowheretomillionaire.com**. Click on "Community." Sign up. Create a profile, introduce yourself. If you'd like, create a video letting us know what you would do to make $10,000 in three days and what you have done to make more money than you ever have while being in service to others. Or just let everyone know where you are and where you'd like to be. Post it. Ask others to help you be accountable to reach your goals. It's that simple.

As your coach, I need you to believe that you only have 72 hours to get real, to forgive, to overcome your fears and doubts, and to take immediate action. Once you do these things, we can get into the practical, how-to-make-money information.

DON'T FORGET ABOUT
facebook
myspace
Linked in
twitter
AND OTHER SOCIAL NETWORKING SITES

The best way to take committed action is to involve friends.

Select ones you think are open to making this journey with you and ask them to buy this book, too. In fact, they can order it now at **www.nowheretomillionaire.com**. Pretend you spent $100,000 for this system — because that's what it's worth to you! If you actually had spent that much, you would pay attention and do everything I ask, wouldn't you?

Explore the process together and challenge each other to dig past the surface so you can discover your true selves and honestly, openly change your lives.

Community is your key to success.

Embarking on this journey alone can result in negativity in those around you — they might have a hard time understanding your experiences. That will hold you back. Work together to change your respective lives, and your success will be faster.

Think of yourself as a newly planted seed, a newly exposed bud who needs to not be consumed by a crow, an ex, a partner, a family member, a friend, or a co-worker. Can you relate? Of course you can. We all have that person in our lives who seems to wait in the wings and suck the very life, the very passion, from our hopes and dreams. Get rid of them now. Look them in the eye and say, "See ya, wouldn't want to be ya!"

You wouldn't plant a garden on a toxic dump, would you? So why are you doing that to yourself?

Open yourself up to the free-ality that you can change dramatically in 72 hours. If you think you can't, then you can't. Tell yourself you can, and you WILL.

If you keep doing what you've been doing, will you be where you want to be?

Are you there now? I doubt it.

If you keep holding on to things that aren't working for you, how much progress do you think you'll make? Why commit to struggling, to being stuck, rigid, hidden, and unfocused, to feeling powerless, unbalanced, without passion or purpose?

Would you leave your hand on a hot stove or would you move it? If a doctor said you had to change your diet immediately or you would die, would you change it? Of course you would! You'd stop at the health-food store the minute you left her office.

Then consider me your doctor. Here's the prognosis:

You are the only person holding you back. Take a risk — look your fears in the face and tell them:

"YOU ARE NOT THE BOSS OF ME. I AM THE BOSS OF ME!"

Don't let fear get in the way of being prosperous and powerful. Want to know the truth about the *current* you? It's boring and on autopilot. I would even venture to say that you are not, right now, living your life purpose. You don't understand what you were put on this earth to do. If you do, terrific, but you're likely not doing much about it, are you?

Look at the people around you, at those with whom you choose to surround yourself. Have you outgrown them? Do they understand you anymore? Are they holding you back from fulfilling your dreams? Let me guess — they complain about everything and fail to see the good in life. That's dangerous — do you know why? Because pretty soon you'll start to do the same. Before you know it, you will be sucked into the same negative pattern and your dreams will slip even farther away.

WENDY POWER kicks the enemy of life in the tush. **WENDY POWER** doesn't believe that misery loves company. **WENDY POWER** will not let you whine, "I'm lonely so this group of friends is the best I can do."

WENDY POWER says, "I don't have to surround myself with complaining, negative friends — we gossip, waste time, feel powerless, blame, eat too many Twinkies, judge others, and don't like ourselves very much."

You may even blame your friends and/or family for making your life so small, unfulfilled, and joyless. You have given your power away for so long that now you may be feeling depressed or hopeless. You may be in a marriage that is no longer healthy or loving, and you make excuses like, "We are staying together for the kids." Or maybe, "How would I pay for things, without him? I know he/she is abusive but I'm stuck and this is the best I can do."

This book will be important for you to reclaim your power and finally be receptive to abundance.

Some people around you may make fun of you, ridicule you, fail to listen to you, and fear you will leave them behind. They are hoping you'll "fail" so you stay down with them, at their depressing levels of mediocrity.

You understand right now that if you don't do something about what you can't stand anymore, you will be permanently resigned, cynical, and apathetic. Deep inside, this scares you. You may not have even owned up to this reality yet or you're denying it even as you read these words.

I can hear your thoughts now: "No, no, that's not me. I don't do that. I don't let others do that to me, I'm my own person." That's B.S.

OWN YOUR POWER NOW.

What do I mean by power? It's your ability to do something with great vitality and strength. I do not mean domination, control, supremacy, to rule, command, or to manipulate.

If you don't do something now, your life will be reduced to bragging about your kids or your pets, weakly watching television and paying down your credit cards because, once again, you bought some product that promised you the easy abs through osmosis, the slim body by sitting on your couch popping chips while watching the video, the instant wealth-building system if you sign your life — and your checking account — over now. You name it, it's out there. I'm sure you've seen it.

Do you know what the saddest thing is? YOU BOUGHT IT!

I bet you never even took "it" out of the box, either. Now you blame the product. It didn't help you lose those extra pounds, did it? You're still not rich, are you? Still haven't found eternal happiness in the perfect mate, have you?

But you never actually used the product, did you? Or, if you did, you tried it once and your lazy self took over and put it back in the box on a shelf. Gee, I wonder why it didn't work?

It's not the product that doesn't work, it's you!

I don't know if this is that defining moment when being who you imagine yourself to be is more interesting to you than retiring on wieners and reading your epitaph: "S/he almost tried...."

Wake up! Now! Here's the cold, hard truth: you either care about making dramatic shifts in your life now or you don't.

Face it, shi(f)t happens.

If you want to change your life in 72 hours, you get to start by identifying and accepting where you are now, then realizing where you really want to be. I guarantee that where you want to be is not where you are right now. The problem you're about to face is the gap between both realities — this is where you need to focus your efforts, on moving from where you are now to where and who you intend to be.

Consider health, love, time, balance, legacy, making a difference in the world — absolutely anything and everything you care about. Ask, *how important is _____ to me on a scale of 1 to 10?* Write down the number. Determine where you are on a scale of 1 to 10, then find the gap.

Don't judge where you are — that's going to change. In order to get where you're going, you have to know where you're starting. We can't build a very good road map if we're missing Point A, can we? That's what you need to find — Point A (where you are) — so you can arrive safely at Point B (where you CHOOSE to be).

Write three easy action steps you can take now in one of the above categories (finance, health, love, etc.), then get out there and do them. Do them today, not tomorrow or next week. Not when you finish what you're working on. Do them now. In fact, stop reading. Write them down and act now.

You have come this far in your commitment to take action and change your life. You have 72 hours and you can't afford one more minute of procrastination.

Start writing:

1. _____

2. _____

3. _____

Three days left to live would give reason enough for you to accelerate your life, your dreams, your purpose, your reason for being born, wouldn't it?

If something is not working yet, you think, "I've got plenty of time." No you don't. Quit thinking that. Right now. You don't have time. Not in this journey, you don't. Time is exactly what you don't have.

We fill our life to the brim with meaningless garbage. Don't we?

**We care about people and things that in the long run —
or in our last 72 hours — don't mean a thing.**

Worry. Doubt. Fear. Blah. Blah. Blah. Being alive is better than being dead, isn't it? I meet a lot of people who appear to be more afraid of being alive than dead. Why are you allowing your thoughts, your beliefs — all of these virus-laden programs that have been running within you — to suck the very life from your being?

Quit giving them power!

Quit handing over your energy and attention to them and allowing them to control who you are. You have the potential to be whoever and whatever you want. Don't you want to be in control of that? If you're not, who is? Wake up and live big now.

Be a leader. Inspire. Motivate. Awaken. Activate yourself and everyone around you to truly live your dream.

Love is the opposite of fear. Both cannot be present at the same moment.

Always choose love. Never choose fear. At least not in this new, improved, three-day life experiment in which you are steeped in a delicious, nourishing soup called Your Life According to You. You deserve the added spice of **WENDY POWER.**

That's it with the pep talk, at least for now. Hopefully I've helped you understand who you need to be to have financial freedom and identify the qualities and characteristics that will become your new power statement, your mantra, your understanding. Our goal throughout this journey is to help you naturally and authentically become the person who embraces organic gifts of abundance.

Take a moment and find your Wendy Power mantra now before you go any further. Now, write this mantra down. Use words that create a new way of being for you to accelerate your success. Words to consider are *loving, powerful, patient, vulnerable, happy*. Below are examples of who you can choose to be:

Are you a powerful, responsible, courageous person?

Are you a passionate, compassionate, creative person?

Are you an unstoppable, loving, take-action-now person?

What are the qualities you embrace that encourage, inspire and activate you to be the super hero(ine) you were born to be?

Make up your own character here based on what you value and what you think or feel it will take to be financially free.

To be a millionaire within three short years, I get to embrace these qualities:

1. _____

2. _____

3. _____

Now put these qualities you just wrote into a powerful sentence.

I am a _____ ,

_____ ,

_____ ,

person, wo/man, leader, or visionary who is financially free.

Here's my sentence: *I am a passionate, compassionate, creative woman.*

Why did I choose that? I felt like I was living my life by reacting to everything. I was shut down and on auto-pilot. Can you relate? I had also been described as tough or arrogant and that is why I wrote this mantra. Sure enough, I quickly took on these characteristics and was never called tough or arrogant again.

Soon strangers and people I knew started to say, "You are so compassionate and understanding. You've got such a huge heart." I have to tell you, that has created a tremendous shift for me. In an intense experiential leadership course where I learned this technique, I was called "the heart of the team." I swear, there was a time months before that when I didn't honestly know what true love was. I always led by my head, not my heart.

I was so shut down that the way I taught myself to nurture and to love was by caring for a little plant. I went through a few at first; I just kept killing them. Eventually, I was able to predict my little plant's needs; I would even sing to it. I made sure it had what it needed to grow and — finally — one started to grow...and kept growing, just like I was. My heart had cracked open.

People in the leadership class at the very end of the six-month course got on their knees and said, "I will follow wherever you lead." That changed my life more than almost anything else. I will remember it for the rest of my life; it will probably be one of the last things I remember as I take my final breath.

This is why I ask you to come up with a statement that reflects who and what you aspire to be, then immediately start acting as though you are that person.

What is your power statement? Who do you intend to be?

Say it out loud. How did that feel? Was it a new sensation? Did you get an uplifting feeling from acting as if you have these qualities now?

Did you doubt it or did you believe it? If you still have doubts, find the times you have exhibited those qualities. Decide to be open now, to really explore what it means to be a powerful, passionate, prosperous person.

- Make cards and put them all over your home, office and car. Say it over and over, especially when you feel weak, insecure, or doubtful.

- Write at least one simple, easy action you will take today so you can experience being that person now.

If you don't act now, when will you? Are you doing what you usually do — a whole lot of nothing? Does that work for you? What results do you get when you don't do anything? Most people won't write the three simple qualities. Are you one of those people? Why?

What scares you so much that you don't even take one single step toward solving your boring, uninspired life challenges? Why does this "thing" have such a hold on you?

Hiding in the security of your "comfort zone" will not get you where you need to go. Taking action *now* will — but it requires courage. People will often reinforce your doubts. Doubt is lack of faith.

Do you have faith in yourself?
Have faith in your abilities. Have faith in yourself.
Believe in yourself. YOUR WORD IS LAW!

Identify where you are and where you want to be. Acknowledge that you will need to change your thoughts, emotions, habits, and actions in order to change the results. Are you open to that? Are you sure?

Awesome. I believe you. Do you believe you?

Not all of your challenges will be resolved in just 72 hours. However, the foundation for resolving them will be firmly put in place. You will make a dent in your universe of fear and lack of focus or balance. You will have a step-by-step millionaire mind-set from which to act. You will be more genuine and authentic.

Do what I ask you to do with urgency — set your desire on fire and make your enthusiasm unstoppable — and we will create dramatic, life-changing results fast.

You will learn wealth and wisdom secrets that have been jealously guarded by the richest people on the planet. Now it's all here in one place, complete with activities to create instant action, leading to dramatic results.

This system is about getting your freedom back, deprogramming old and limiting beliefs, outsourcing your life, finding balance, sharpening your focus, and following through. It's about how to create a millionaire mind-set without sabotaging yourself. Mostly, it's about how to radically reinvent your relationship with money, love, and health.

I want you to become your own boss and hire others to do most — if not all — of the work. If you are facing foreclosure, bankruptcy, or have been laid off, I will help you build your confidence, overcome your fears or doubts, and help you stop looking for a job and create your own business.

If that seems impossible, or if you have lost faith, I understand. I am here to hold your hand so we make it through these challenging times together. It is time to recession-proof your life and to open up your heart.

This book is about the mind/heart opulent connection where you are given permission to be yourself and to be rich in every aspect of the word.

Enjoy! Pass this book on! Like you, I also have a goal. Mine is to be a best-selling author. I can get there a lot faster, a lot easier, with your support and enthusiastic referrals. Let's tingle the world together!

Tweet this... Your Followers Will Love It!

Visit me today at: **www.nowheretomillionaire.com**
www.facebook.com/wendyrobbins
www.twitter.com/wendyrobbins
www.askwendynow.com
www.tingletribe.com

When you know you are serious about taking action and creating results in your life, visit **www.nowheretomillionaire.com** to access a free coaching session!

PRACTICE

1. List the five things you need to do if you only had 72 hours to live. Then, go out and fulfill each of the items on that list. Pay attention to what is important to you now — trust your intuition. This could very well reveal your life's purpose.

2. Make a list of what you will do to make the $10,000 to save your friend's life. Do at least one of those things today. This will show you your true interests and passions.

3. Create your **WENDY POWER** mantra and post it everywhere so you easily memorize and believe it. Focus on being the change you envision for yourself.

4. Do three things that will save you time, then use that newly found time to celebrate wildly. HINT: Enough with the texting; e-mails can wait, and Facebook certainly isn't going anywhere.

5. Find at least five people or friends to mastermind with using this book and ask them to hold you accountable so you actually do what you say you will. Commit to working with them; enroll them in your dream and you help to ensure their dreams come true as well.

6. Figure out where you are now in all aspects of your life and identify where you want to be. On a scale of 1 to 10, where is the gap? Who do you need to be, and what will you do to close the gap fast? Consider the following: finances, time, love, giving back to community, spirituality, fun, health, personal power, passion, life purpose, etc. Commit to making immediate changes today.

CHAPTER 2: How to Get Committed

I want you to answer some questions.

Take your time and don't rush through them. I think that your answers may very well surprise or shock you.

They will also help you change quickly. As you go through the list, if you find yourself resisting or spending too much time on an answer, stop. Take a deep breath and look inside yourself to find the truth.

Remind yourself that you are open to this adventure and to these changes you want — and need — to make because you are challenging yourself in every aspect of your life.

Answer these questions knowing that you — and only you — will see the answer. If you are comfortable, share them or mastermind with others you trust, those you know can help you get to the depths of your core.

If you don't want to write in this book, go ahead and grab a notebook, your laptop, a secret journal — whatever you're most comfortable with — and record your answers there.

Ready? Let's go.

Please write down your honest answers to the following questions:

1. To what do you commit over the next three days?

   _____

   _____

2. What breakthroughs do you expect will happen?

   _____

   _____

3. What will your excuses be if you don't create a breakthrough?

   _____

   _____

4. What will it take to accomplish what you want to achieve?

   _____

   _____

5. What's not working in your life right now?

   _____

   _____

6. Where are you stuck in your life?

   _____

   _____

7. What negative feedback do you hear that is most hurtful?

   _____

   _____

8. What negative energy are you holding on to and why?

   _____

   _____

9. What motivates you?

    _____

    _____

10. What support can I provide so you feel safe and trust me to coach you to have an extraordinary life?

    _____

    _____

11. Are you living your potential? If not, why?

    _____

    _____

12. What is possible for you?

    _____

    _____

13. How is fear stopping you? What do you fear most?

    _____

    _____

14. What do you usually do when you are afraid?

    _____

    _____

15. Why is your life worth living?

    _____

    _____

16. Do you feel powerful? If not, why?

    _____

    _____

17. Are you willing to feel powerful by taking action on what you learn?

_____

_____

18. What are you grateful for?

_____

_____

19. What is making you feel trapped?

_____

_____

20. How do you avoid honest communication?

_____

_____

21. How can I open you up when you are shut down?

_____

_____

22. Who were you not allowed to be as a child?

_____

_____

23. What were you not allowed to have?

_____

_____

24. What decisions did you make about yourself as a child that you are still holding on to?

_____

_____

25. What defenses have you put up to survive or to stay safe?

_____

_____

26. What don't you like about yourself? Why?

_____

_____

27. What happens when you meet others who have the characteristics you don't like in yourself?

_____

_____

28. How much of your time is spent on others rather than yourself?

_____

_____

29. What is your power mantra? (Go to previous chapter to review if you have already forgotten or skipped that exercise.)

_____

_____

30. What does **WENDY POWER** mean to you?

_____

_____

Now that you've answered these questions, you've identified some past issues that may be stalling your potential. Once you identify and are honest with yourself, change can happen — but only if you are open to it. Remember, you can't eliminate your problems with the same thoughts that created them.

Since we are spending quite a bit of time together, I would like to tell you a story about myself.

HOW TO TINGLE THE WORLD

I have "tingled" the world and given a million people orgasms.

What?!?!

Years ago, I — along with an amazing partner — developed something called The Tingler™. *InStyle* magazine said that The Tingler™ head massager was an "orgasm for the head."

InStyle featured a blurb about The Tingler™ alongside a picture of Gwyneth Paltrow enjoying one. In two weeks, we sold 25,000 of them, grossing $450,000. What followed became a multimillion-dollar business. We had 5,600 distributors and a story on CNN that exploded our international sales — so we really did tingle the world.

More than twenty years of studying personal development, motivational, and inspirational books paid off. I went to seminars, workshops, and took part in teleclass calls.

I could have earned a gold medal just from training my mind to win the high jump, the breaststroke, and the marathon of successfully selling converted hangers into something pleasurable.

What exactly is The Tingler™, you ask?

I'll give you a brief history of how our product (named the best invention of the 21st century by *Elle* magazine, by the way) came to life.

My soon-to-be business partner massaged my head one day with a homemade device that made my toes curl. In that moment of bliss, shaking in delight, I knew all our dreams of getting rich were about to be realized.

The following morning, I went to the hardware store and found plumbing parts. We used hangers with dabs of glue on the tips to create our very first prototype.

I went to a trendy store in Santa Monica, California — a place frequented by celebrities who didn't think twice about spending $400 on pairs of ripped-up,

stained jeans and $1,000 for mismatched shoes. It was a crazy-enough reality that I figured this would be the perfect place to sell our Tingler.

I went into Fred Segal's and asked to meet with the owner so I could tingle her. She screamed so loudly I could see where her tonsils would have been.

"GET OUT!!!!!!"

I stood there waiting for my ears to stop ringing, but I didn't move. I was on a mission — a little screaming and garlic breath weren't going to stop me.

"Wow, you're really uptight! I bet you could use a little head massage. It's very relaxing."

She ultimately gave in, and — still a bit rigid — let me rub her head with the copper spider until her shoulders stopped climbing up beyond her ears. I could see she had a neck, a smile, a giggle...then full-fledged laughter.

On the spot, she ordered 144 Tinglers. One hundred and forty-four!!!! We were in business.

Of course, there were a few challenges:

1. I didn't know how to take an order. I had never done it.

2. We didn't accept credit cards.

3. We didn't have product or a manufacturer.

The first two challenges almost stopped everything. Here's our solution:

1. I got a napkin and her business card and wrote out the order.

2. I admitted we were new to the business world and needed her to pay by check. She agreed.

3. I told her the order would take six to eight weeks.

She accepted the terms. I then walked around to what seemed like every store in Santa Monica and sold hundreds more Tinglers. In gratitude and with a hint of disbelief, I walked to the ocean and watched the sunset as dolphins leapt and played.

The next day, my business partner and I set out to find bobby-pin manufacturers who could provide the tips we needed — so instead of literally scratching the head, The Tingler™ would actually massage it. We found two people in the country who made them; everyone else was in China.

One couldn't do it. The other was in Rhode Island; we were in California. We flew to Rhode Island, rented an RV, and went on an adventure to convince someone we had never met to make Tinglers for us — even though we weren't sure exactly how to make them, what they would cost, or how many would sell. Good business plan, right?

We found a family-run factory that made jewelry. They loved a challenge so they said yes. We told them that we needed our first order of 500 in four weeks and 500 more soon after that. They said, "No problem." This was in October. We would have product for Christmas.

Then we had to break the news that we couldn't pay them until our customers paid us. We didn't feel the need to also mention that we were already $10,000 deep in credit-card debt.

It didn't matter — they believed in us. We believed in us.

The order was slightly late, but it arrived in time for us to still be Santa's vixens — giving the best head anyone had ever experienced.

All of our customers sold out in days and ordered more. We were a success.

Blythe Danner and her daughter, Gwyneth Paltrow,
were the very first people to buy a Tingler. Then Hank Azaria
bought 25 of them for everyone on The Simpsons. Doh!

We even got a call from a makeup artist with a woman giggling in the background. Julia Roberts was tingling Catherine Zeta-Jones because John Cusack, who got one from Kate Hudson, who got one from her mom, Goldie Hawn, all loved The Tingler™.

We became the new Prozac for the stars.

Months later we found ourselves in New York City at *Rolling Stone* magazine pitching The Tingler™. We were invited to the premiere of a movie starring Angelina Jolie and Denzel Washington. There we were strutting down the red carpet, cameras snapping away, and all we could hear was:

"The Tingler! It's the Tingler Girls!!!!!"

We tingled celebrity heads, snuck into Hollywood parties, were brought out on stages in front of thousands of fans, invited onto movie sets and met with writers, producers, and actors to help incorporate The Tingler™ into their story lines.

The Tingler™ was featured on *Sex and the City*, *Miss Congeniality 2*, *Legally Blonde 2*, *Will and Grace*, *Ellen*, *The Rosie O'Donnell Show*, *The Montel Williams Show*, CNN, and MTV. We were on countless other television shows and radio programs, featured in newspapers and magazines like *InStyle*, *Glamour*, *Jane*, *Redbook*, *Ladies Home Journal*, *Maxim*, and *Elle*.

In fact, we still get calls from friends and people who have seen The Tingler™ in a movie or TV show.

In the background, there were difficult, expensive, and painful lessons.

This is the part of the story where
I tell you NOT to do exactly what we did.

Managing money was never my strong suit. Deep inside I didn't feel truly deserving of my newfound wealth. In some ways, I took it for granted and just thought it would always be there. We were making $1 million to $2 million a year and only paid ourselves $50,000 to $100,000. Sometimes we didn't take a salary so we could pay others who said they could help make our business even more successful than it already was. Sadly, most never followed through.

Our biggest problem was that we needed another manufacturer who had connections to China. We found someone who said he could help, so we met with him. He appeared to be a nice man, he shared our values and our vision and he seemed to be a perfect candidate for our second manufacturer. Not only that, he was going to handle all of our customer service and fulfillment.

Our next step was to hand over our database of established customers, which is when things started to go terribly awry. It didn't take too long for us to realize that we had partnered with the wrong person. *His* next step was to take our database and contact some of our customers to tell them that we were no longer in business. He then proceeded to take our product and put his information on it instead of ours.

The nightmare quickly unfolded as he told our clients that if they continued to do business with us he would sue them. This happened just days before Thanksgiving. My mother didn't speak to me for almost a year for missing that dinner.

Fortunately, we had already built solid relationships with all of our clients. We managed to contact every one of our customers within 24 hours to let them know we were still in business and that they could continue to buy The Tingler™ from us...without winding up in a courtroom.

Prior to this, we had started conversations with manufacturers in China, so we contacted them again to secure them as our overseas manufacturer. After many days of tiring work, we had our manufacturers, we had our product — and we also had competition.

Our opposition was able to get some of our biggest retail chains to order instead from his company at a reduced price. It was stressful and depressing. He even fought our patents, though we won. We ended up winning in a lot of ways: we learned to stand up for ourselves and fight back and we learned how to be business women. We also learned profound lessons of persistence.

We learned:

DON'T MESS WITH ME — THIS AIN'T MY FIRST RODEO.

We emerged with a few more gray hairs and wrinkles, but also with a brilliant life lesson: *forgiveness*.

Through all of this, I was still left with the idea that making money was painful and so not worth it. Even with the headache and heartache of the experience behind us, more problems popped up at every turn.

Overpriced accountants and financial planners resulted in a loss of hundreds of thousands of dollars — not to mention sleepless nights over late or missing orders. Copper prices skyrocketed 100 percent and we had to lower our price.

Buyers weren't traveling to trade shows as much so our sales began to decline. The novelty of the product had also worn off, which meant not as much press coverage to drive sales.

In spite of all of this, we do still see royalties for our past work.

This is called passive income. That's what you want in your life, too.

Luckily, there are some people who still haven't heard of The Tingler™ and fall in love when they discover it. The next time you are in the market for a head massager, make sure to look for The Tingler™ label. In fact, ask your local stores to carry it or get it now online at **www.nowheretomillionaire.com**. When you purchase it online from this site — and if you are serious about wanting a mentor — I will throw in a free coaching session with a coach from my team!

Did you know that Disney went bankrupt six times before Disneyland was built? Most millionaires lose it all and get it back because they have the mind-set and the skills to do it all over again. They could do it and I knew I could, too.

You might be asking yourself why I'm telling you this story of heartache and loss. I'm telling you because I want you to know that I have experienced what it is like to go from mountains of debt to making millions — making a lot of mistakes along the way. I want to help you avoid those same mistakes.

I want you to know that I understand where you are now,
and where you can and will be.

I sabotaged every good opportunity that came my way until my back was against the wall. Whatever I chose had to be different from what I had done in the past. I kept lots of journals about what was working and what wasn't. I worked endless, compulsive hours until a friend reminded me to work hard because the people on welfare depend on me!

I needed to train my thoughts to stop obsessing about the same old negative stories. I knew I needed to listen to my inner selves — the challenge was which one to listen to: the one who believed fully in me or the one who doubted that I could succeed? The latter had such a loud, practical, dramatic flair that if I listened to her I wouldn't have to work hard at all. Why even bother starting?

I felt like a failure because opportunities kept slipping through my fingers. I would come so close to a deal that promised the prosperity I needed, and then it would suddenly disappear.

Can you relate?

My savings were shrinking, and I started only buying products that were on sale. I learned to do with less, and I was convinced that I would never be successful again. Meanwhile, people thought I was still a millionaire and loved me for the favors they thought they could get.

I struggled to speak about money because it wasn't coming my way. I started to spiral into victim mode and lived a nonstop pity party. Of course, no one showed up — after all, who wants to hang out at a party like that? "Welcome! Grab a seat and a great big glass of negativity!"

When I realized how unproductive my attitude had become, I taught myself to shift from victimized to responsible. I turned my thoughts upside-down, from negative to positive. I wavered, gave in to weakness, and sometimes didn't expect enough of myself. That's when I realized the only way out was in.

I took a shovel to my soul and kept digging. What is my purpose? Who am I? What is my legacy? Am I loving openly without holding back? Am I making a difference? If I died today, would I be complete? Am I living fully to and beyond my potential? Basic questions, contemplated from an expansive place, led to my realization that it's not about me.

These lessons were more valuable than any dollar I had ever earned.

I had to go back to basics — you know, the core lessons that all the personal-growth, motivational, and inspirational teachers talk to you about? I counseled with millionaires and a billionaire, and wrote down everything I learned from them after my fall. All of them could relate and had their own transitional stories to share with me. I no longer felt alone — I now had a community.

I became a success coach. Personally, I found that rather funny because there I was telling people what to do when I couldn't even do it myself. I must have known what I was doing because I went on to be voted "Best Coach" for the fastest growing Personal Development company in the world. They had about 200 coaches at that time. My testimonials were glowing.

This helped build my confidence and forced me to realize that I could do it again. It was time to study the different ways to make a lot of money working for yourself without having experience or a large initial investment.

For three years I've hosted a popular radio show and have interviewed masters of the 21st century from spiritual, health, financial, and environmental sectors. These conversations are heard by half a million people weekly and have inspired me to learn and teach everything I know about making money — all while loving every aspect of my life.

I was once interviewing best-selling author and *Oprah and Friends* radio host Marianne Williamson. I admitted that I was playing too small of a game with my life — I was hiding out and not living my life purpose. It was time to have the courage to affect millions of lives by being myself and being honest. All she needed to say was, "You go, girl." Simple, right? So I say to you:

YOU GO, GIRL!

What did I do to play a much bigger game with my life? I used the techniques I am sharing with you in this book. I answered the questions you will answer in this book. I visualized being on television and coaching millions to take on their lives and act on their dreams in spite of all the odds against them.

Six months later, I received a call from a casting director, asking if I wanted to be on television. I said, "YES!!!"

Like most things in my life at that time, it was not as simple as saying "Yes."It turned out there was a lot of competition and a lot of people needing to say "Yes" back to me.

Another two months went by and — finally — a day before I was leaving for Europe, I was told that I got the job.

Now, I'm starring in a TV series with Kelly Ripa where I get to coach women inventors and help them realize their dreams. If that isn't my dream job, I'm not sure what is. Plus, I'm now participating with some of my favorite mentors in a movie distributed by the same people who published *The Secret*.

You don't need the secret — you need answers.

To your prosperity and to you tingling the world!

PRACTICE

1. How will you tingle the world?

2. What idea, product, or service are you bringing to market?

3. It's selfish not to make your brilliance available to the world. Realize that now.

4. Are you ready to shift your thinking? Are you willing to be coached? To create your "free-ality"?

5. What is the story of you, regarding money and success? Where are you now?

6. Meet other like-minded people by clicking on "Community" at: **www.nowheretomillionaire.com.**

7. Which celebrities can you inspire to pitch your product or service — or at least to use it in public so that it's picked up in the press? Make a list of names, then set a goal to get at least one photo.

HOW TO MEET CELEBRITIES AND HAVE THEM WORK WITH YOU

Use your **WENDY POWER** to meet everyone you have ever admired! There are lots of ways to meet and work with celebrities. I have done it through PR people, bodyguards, hair and makeup people, agents, by being friends on Facebook, or by following them on Twitter. You can often have direct access to them (unless they have an assistant handling this for them online).

If you are passionate, persistent, have an amazing product, and are willing to give back to your community, there will be a celebrity willing to endorse or use your product.

If the celebrity has a large fan base, you could be a millionaire faster than you originally thought. A picture of Gwyneth Paltrow using our product in *InStyle* magazine with a mention of other stars using it meant $450,000 in sales in less than two weeks!

Never underestimate the power of stardom! Look at the George Foreman grill — would it have been as successful without George?

You can also go to my website to get information on how to find almost any celebrity. I have access to a huge database. Be genuine, sincere, and respect everyone's time. Remember that they are busy.

Do your homework and know the celebrities' likes and dislikes. What causes do they support? Do they endorse other products? What's in it for them?

If you have a product you want a celebrity to pitch, contact her or his agent or manager. It will cost you, but often not as much as you would think.

Kelly Ripa is so generous and amazing to work with. One time we were shooting late at night — 10:30 or so — and Kelly was leaving for vacation the next morning. After the shoot, she jetted out, returning a minute later to give me a hug before leaving again. That kind of consideration is huge! After we were done with the final shoot of the first season, Kelly sent a nice bottle of wine with a handwritten note:

Dear Wendy, Thank you so much for being such an instrumental part of Homemade Millionaire! Your positive energy both on camera and off was much appreciated. The impact you had on the ladies was evident. You really improved their lives! Hope to work with you in the future. Best, Kelly

Remember to be kind to everyone you work with — send cards or small gifts, telling them how amazing they are. Don't we all appreciate that?

PRACTICE

1. Fantasize about your favorite celebrity promoting your product, service, or idea.

2. How did you meet them?

3. What did you say to inspire them to say "Yes!" to you?

4. How much money did you both make as a result?

5. Did doors open up faster because of this?

6. How did **WENDY POWER** help you overcome your fears and shyness? Did your mantra help you? Who are you again?

CHAPTER 3: Who Else Wants to Be a Millionaire?

Face it. There are two ways to be a millionaire: become one or marry one.

I say, "Why marry a millionaire? Just be one!"

Let's acknowledge a sexist fact. We typically think of a woman marrying a rich man and *voilà*, she's a multi-millionaire. That's not always the case.

John Kerry married the Heinz heiress. Hey, if ketchup can make someone that much money, imagine what's possible for you! Look at John McCain; he didn't even know how many houses he owned. I guess his wealthy wife forgot to send him the memo. Who doesn't know how many houses they own? We likely all do — we're still paying them off...and, oh yeah, we pay attention.

Here's a compelling truth: women need more money than men. Why?

So we can buy more shoes, purses, lipstick, Botox, and a boob job to keep that rich man happy? *I don't think so.*

It's because we generally live longer than men, make less money, and are far more likely to be a single parent raising a family on one income.

In the U.S., women comprise 87 percent of the impoverished elderly.

We're taught that a man will take care of us, so we invest ourselves in that handsome Wall Street broker. Broker is right!

Don't depend on another man or woman to take care of you. You — and you alone — are 100 percent responsible for you and your choices. All of them, even the ones that don't make sense.

Take this survey to see if you've got what it takes to be a millionaire. Answer true or false, and don't spend too much time pondering your responses:

1. I depend upon others to make choices for me.

2. I am too scared to take action.

3. I don't think it's spiritual to make money.

4. I overspend and am always in debt.

5. I avoid money. I don't pay my bills on time. I have no idea how much money I have.

6. I think money is a hassle. It takes too much work.

7. I hate my boss, my job and my co-workers — but this is as good as it gets.

8. I still believe in what my parents told me about money.

9. I'd be rich if I had married Billionaire Bob D. Vulture.

10. If it's to be, it's up to me.

If you answered "true" to most of questions 1 through 9, I'm afraid the journey is going to be hard for you. You would be living in:

WENDY POWERLESS (Wasting Energy Now Daily, Yes?!)

Your energy is like a bank account. It is either your vast richness or it is depleted and bankrupt. Your energy is your life.

We waste time by being mindless, powerless, passionless, stressed, resistant, and/or suffering. When you find yourself in the **WENDY POWERLESS** state — *simply stop.*

Realize you have a choice and choose one that reflects **WENDY POWER**. Your emotional, energetic, and physical bank account will be opulent and overflowing, while you use the least amount of doubtful, angry, or sad energy.

If you don't change your beliefs now, you will never be a millionaire.

If you are still sitting around waiting for someone with a seemingly bottomless bank account to cure your money woes, you are delusional.

Don't believe me? Here are two examples of men and money:

1. A man proudly told his friend, "I'm responsible for making my wife a millionaire."

   "Well, what was she before she married you?" the friend asked.

   "A billionaire."

2. A man who loved money more than just about anything, said to his wife just before he died, "When I die, I want you to take all my money and put it in the casket with me. I want to take my money to the afterlife with me."

   When he died, she did what she had promised, came over with the money box, and put it in the casket. Then the undertakers locked the casket down and rolled it away. A concerned friend said, "Girl, I know you weren't foolish enough to put all that money in there with your husband!"

   She said, "I promised him that I was going to put that money in that casket with him." "You mean to tell me you really put that money in the casket with him!!!!?" "I sure did," said the wife. "I wrote him a check."

We are only a couple of hours into your process and you are about to be a millionaire on paper. That's a start, right?

DO THIS!!!

Speaking of checks, I'd like you to do something right now.

1. **Write yourself a check for $1 million.**

2. **Date it a year from now.**

3. **Imagine it's real and that you will be able to cash it.**

4. **Put it in your wallet.**

When I was $10,000 in credit-card debt, I wrote myself a check for $1 million. In two years, I could have cashed that check. I never quit. I trusted, and knew the business would make the million. It was beyond faith.

Something clicked, like a 10,000-pound magnet attracting silver and gold to me. That's what it feels like — you are magnetic.

What you desire moves toward you without effort. It clicks. It locks in.

The opulent energy that is everything — including you — gives you a gift that is for you and for the greatest good of all. Now, what you thought and think about is brought about.

Jim Carrey wrote a check to himself for $20 million and went on to become the first actor to ever make $20 million for a movie.

Write the check to yourself right now.

Do it. Feel great and powerful and trust that it will be yours. Treat it as though it's real — because it is.

Write it out and celebrate. Remember that a hangover is simply the wrath of grapes.

A one-dollar bill met a hundred-dollar bill and said, "Hey, where've you been? I haven't seen you around here much."

The hundred answered, "I've been hanging out at the casinos, went on a cruise around the world, and did the rounds of the ship. I went back to the United States for a while, went to some concerts, the theater, the mall, that kind of stuff. How about you?"

The one-dollar bill said, "Oh, the same old stuff...church, church, church."

This joke reminds me to remind you to tithe. I invite you to pay it forward. Practice the law of circulation, attraction, and resonance. If you hold on to your money, it's just that — held and stagnant.

Financial freedom is free.

When the media tells us there is not enough, you don't have to believe it. We can give to each other. We can barter. We can trust there is enough for all of us. Go online and search the term "barter." You'll be amazed by what pops up!

What random act of kindness are you performing today? The more you do, the richer you are. Pay the toll for the person behind you. Buy a stranger an ice cream cone. Tell an 80-year-old woman she looks sexy.

PRACTICE

1. Write a check to yourself for $1 million. Date it, carry it in your wallet, and believe you can cash it.

2. Tithe — give generously today even if you feel like you don't have the money. Trust that you do.

3. Be kind to strangers today. It can be a compliment, buying them a flower, leaving an anonymous note or helping them out in any way that delights you.

4. Live in gratitude. What are you grateful for? What do you appreciate? Start and end your days in contemplation and your life will change. Journal about it daily and your focus will shift, bringing you more of what you like.

5. Right now, act as if you are a millionaire. Be it. See it. What is your lifestyle like? How do you grow your money so easily?

6. Realize now that the universe can easily bring you a dollar or a million — it's no more difficult to do either. The universe is abundant and can bring you the opportunities, the clients, the work, and the money if you bring the joy, the appreciation, the surrender, the acceptance, the gratitude, and the enthusiasm. Are you open to doing your part?

REALITY CHECK

If you are still contemplating marrying someone for money, remember that marriage, to him, is an expensive laundry and housecleaning service while he works and YOU raise the family. Got that? Let me repeat it.

YOU raise the family.

Housework, home schooling, and other unpaid work in the U.S. is worth at least $11 trillion — almost 50 percent of the world's gross domestic product. What this means is that women are missing out on Social Security, pensions, and access to public services.

Poverty means having little or no income. Of the elderly living in poverty, three out of four are women. Eighty percent of the women were not poor when their husbands were alive.

Approximately seven out of ten women will, at some point, live in poverty.

A lot of women are getting short-term, part-time, or contract work. This means no health insurance or pension benefits.

Even when a woman gets a J.O.B. (Just Over Broke), she is often paid less than men. Worldwide, women's wages are 73 to 77 percent of a man's.

Assuming a woman has retirement income, she is usually the primary caretaker of the home — which means she has less time to work outside of the home. Not only that, women have close to 15 fewer years in the workforce than men. That fact — combined with lower wages — means a woman's retirement benefits are about one-quarter that of a man's. Pretty scary, huh?

These are facts from the National Center for Women and Retirement Research (NCWRR). Changes have been written into law in the U.S. that demand equal pay for men and women — maybe we'll start to see new realities. Yet there is a long "herstory" of lower pay. The collective, ongoing damage from being underpaid will take time to correct.

I have an issue with these statistics — the story that goes with the numbers is often forgotten or untold. I'd like to invite you to take a moment now and realize this could be you, your mom, your aunt, your grandma, your godmother, your neighbor, the woman who owns your favorite cafe, or the homeless woman you pass on the street.

Fifty-eight percent of female baby boomers have less than $10,000 in retirement. Only 10 to 20 percent of female baby boomers will be financially secure in their retirement.

These are women who were born full of dreams, none of which included being broke, fearful, or insecure.

How can we be secure if we keep doing what we have been doing? What are we doing now that doesn't seem to work? It's time for change, right? It's time to do something new — now!

Ninety-five percent of all U.S. citizens over the age of 65 are broke.

This is no time for a whine break. It may, however, be time to cuddle up with an expensive bottle of wine and some snacks as we solve this challenge together.

I was in New York for six weeks during the "Wall Street Crash of 2008." At Zabar's Deli, I was quietly minding my own business (sorta), eavesdropping on a divorced mother giving advice to her unemployed daughter: "Get rich the old fashioned way — marry it. Never sell yourself for cash, take stocks, bonds, and oil wells. Dress on credit and undress for cash. Marry for money and divorce for the same reason."

I immediately imagined the daughter taking the advice and marrying a man who eventually tells his marriage counselor, "My credit card was stolen but I decided not to report it because the thief was spending less than my wife did."

Fifty percent of all marriages end in divorce. What's the number one thing couples fight about? You guessed it: *MONEY.*

We've all heard the jokes, but bear with me for a moment. Take a second and read them again. Look for the truth in each:

A woman said to her husband, "I was a fool when I married you." He said, "Yes, dear, but I was in love and didn't notice."

"I haven't spoken with my wife in 18 months. I don't like to interrupt her."

"I married Mr. Right. I just didn't know his first name was Always."

You think of them differently now, don't you?

As I said, 50 percent of marriages end in divorce. And who typically ends up with the children after a divorce? Yep, the woman. In the first year after a divorce, a woman's standard of living drops an average of 73 percent.

A prenuptial agreement at the altar would be more honest if it stated, "I'll do everything for you. You'll become too demanding and needy, fulfilling none of my needs. We'll fight about money and never having enough. I'll eventually leave and blame you for everything. I do."

Let's say you are part of the rare 50 percent of baby boomers who stay married. You will likely outlive your husband by 10 to 20 years. You will stay in the workforce at least 74 years due to inadequate financial savings and pension coverage. The stress of this "reality" will shorten your life. *Yuck!*

Women — goddesses! — it looks like 5 percent of us will have massive, passive, residual income — while 95 percent of us will become a greeter at WalMart or dependent upon someone else to do it for us.

As of this writing, the government figures that an income of $30,000 a year makes you financially independent. How many of you are trying — or have tried — to live on $30,000 a year? It's possible, but it sure isn't easy, is it? Throw some kids into the mix and it becomes a whole lot more difficult.

Given this statistic, wouldn't you think that younger women would want to catch a clue rather then a bouquet?!

Consider these facts. In the USA:

- Women-owned businesses employ approximately 27 million people.

- Women own 48 percent of all businesses in the United States — that is 9.1 million businesses.*

- Women business owners contribute more than $3.6 trillion to the marketplace each year. Women account for more than 70 percent of consumer spending.*

- 55 percent of women provide half or more of their household's income, yet 48 million women — 80 percent of all women in the workforce — earn less than $25,000 a year. Only 3 percent of women-owned businesses make $1 million a year or more.

(*Facts from "The National Foundation for Women Business Owners")

My mission is to change all of that. How many hours a week do you think these women work? How many of them do you think are raising children? How many do you think would say that their husband is far needier or more spoiled than the children? Here's the reality: they are dealing with a huge amount of stress. Here's another reality: they can work less, outsource most of it, and make even more money from home or anywhere they want.

Let's not be too hard on ourselves. It wasn't until 1975 that women in the U.S. were able to have credit cards and open bank accounts in their own names and without a male cosigner. Crazy, huh?!

By the way, there are — at the time of this writing — ten self-made women billionaires in the world. Oprah Winfrey and J.K Rowling are two who have amazing rags-to-riches stories.

J.K. Rowling, author of the Harry Potter series, used to do most of her writing at cafes because she couldn't afford to keep her home warm. The single mom — once on welfare — would write on napkins because she couldn't afford paper. She is now a billionaire.

Maybe I need to call my book *Why Marry a Billionaire? Just Be One!*

Okay, so I've told a tale of potential futures. You can keep doing what you've been doing or you can do things differently. It's your choice. I am showing you the pain so you are motivated to be, do, and have a different story. When the mind spins with the negative possibilities, it's often time to take a moment and quiet it.

Many of us "try" to meditate. We sit still for two minutes and wonder why it's not bringing the peace of mind we were promised as we worry, fret, and focus on the future and the past all at once.

I invite you to relax. Be present — that's the gift you deserve. You can do that by simply breathing. As you inhale, say "IN," and as you exhale, say "OUT." Doing that forces you to think of nothing else. Your mind will be occupied and happy it has something to do. Try it now.

You'll get better as you practice. When your mind wanders, bring it back gently to "IN" or "OUT." That's it. Uncomplicate everything and realize that there is something bigger than you available to you now. That is the energy you want to start a conversation with. You can also say "thinking," because that is all you are doing.

The only thoughts you need to embrace are those that are in the present. Choose sparkly ones that energize and make you smile.

Can you be one of the amazing rags-to-riches stories of women who solve problems for their family and create a multimillion-dollar business? You can be a mentor to others. Do you see that for yourself?

Drama is in our blood — we are drawn to it, we thrive on it. Let's create dramatic success for you in the 21st century.

You have to love drama. It's like listening to a friend say, "You're not going to believe what she said to me!" Even though you know you need to stay out of this gossip, the drama-loving part of you can't control itself...so you gush out, "Do tell!!!!"

Girlfriend, you don't need the gossip, the negativity, the fear, the I cant's, I shouldn'ts, I'll fails, or any other unhealthy, unnecessary drama.

You can and you will do this!

Breathe. You are safe and well cared for. You have permission to be rich and wholly successful. Infinity is contained in you. The eternal breathes you.

"When circumstances have compelled you to be a little disturbed, return to yourself quickly and do not continue out of tune longer than the compulsion lasts, for you will be more the master of the harmony by continually returning to it."
— Marcus Aurelius

PRACTICE

1. Do you believe you are safe and well cared for?

2. Do you believe you are rich?

3. Are you usually present, or focused on the past or the future?

4. Are you dependent upon a mate to be rich?

5. How is that working for you (even if it's just a fantasy)?

6. What will it take for you to accept that you can easily be a millionaire and love yourself, and another, in healthy ways?

7. Practice breathing while saying "In" and "Out." Notice how it keeps you present. Do this many times daily for the rest of your life.

8. When you think crazy thoughts, say the word "thinking" out loud. That's all that's happening — and you don't need to believe your thoughts. Once you say "thinking," they'll know you are on to them.

9. Contemplate this: who is the thinker behind your thoughts? Witness your thoughts without directly identifying with them. Don't label them as good or bad; the voice in your head is not the real you. We are the stuff of stars — we are eternal. Access that wisdom and be free! Give the eternal source of all a good time living through you as you.

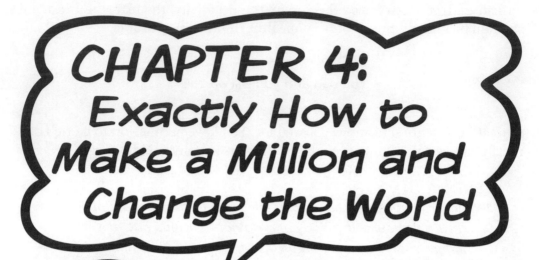

CHAPTER 4: Exactly How to Make a Million and Change the World

In the 1920s and 1930s, Napoleon Hill interviewed some of the richest individuals on the planet. After 500 interviews, he developed 13 steps anyone could follow in order to be rich. The book is called *Think and Grow Rich*. Below is a recap of these 13 pioneering principles. I will expand on them as we make this trip together.

THOUGHTS

So you want to make $1 million. You want to change the world. You want to have fun. You want to love yourself. You want to love others. You want to be healthy and balanced. What you think and thank, you bring about. Thoughts are things — they become your reality.

Concentrate your thoughts on productive activities.

No, checking Facebook and e-mails doesn't count. Spend 45 minutes working on activities that bring you the most money quickly, then take a break to clear your head. Stretch. Exercise. Daydream. Rest for 15 minutes and then work for 45 minutes. Then rest again for 15. Your mind focuses best in 45-minute chunks.

Stay positive and be obsessive — as long as it's about income-producing things. Focus on making that $1 million and changing the world by changing yourself. Kick those negative thoughts to the curb; they won't deliver what you need. Here's a scary statistic: 90 percent or more of what you are thinking right now is negative.

Test this out. Shut up for two minutes and just listen to the thoughts in your mind. What are you saying to yourself?

Pay attention to anything you say to yourself that isn't helping you move forward. Encourage thoughts that support or activate your dreams, and stop listening to the ones that don't.

ACTIVITIES

1. Monitor your thoughts — are they healthy or unhealthy?

2. Do you believe you deserve to be a millionaire or a billionaire and can change the world?

3. Ask for what you want now and truly believe that you can do it. Be prepared and open to receive what you want.

4. Stay strong, focused, and positive. Stop believing the negative thoughts and voices *right now*.

DESIRE

Your desire for what you want needs to burn with enthusiastic fire and passion. You are desire on fire! Commit to your dream and then experience it. Imagine yourself fulfilling your desires. Think about how that would look and feel.

What are your dreams and desires? When do you want to accomplish them? What do you plan to give in return? Really think about these questions and write down your answers. Read what you've written with energy and passion, out loud, several times a day. That is the key most people forget — the one that keeps you accountable, on target, and positive.

Here's an example, if you're not sure what I'm asking you to do: *I easily make, keep and grow $1 million by (Month) (Day) and (Year). I give 10 percent to charity, offer exceptional value to my clients, and get referrals daily so my business grows easily and joyfully.*

If that was your desire, imagine it happening for you! Exciting, huh?! You want to feel it emotionally and passionately. The more you feel it happening — as if it *has happened* — the faster it seems to materialize.

It doesn't matter that you're just starting out on this journey — forget about that. Experience your dreams; pretend they are real at this moment. Appreciate how that makes you feel. Enjoy the sensation of your purpose being fulfilled.

Close your eyes and know that you are a deserving millionaire.

Push your brain across the line from imaginary into reality, because that will be your reality. You *will* be a deserving and generous millionaire.

PRACTICE

1. Determine what is most important to you and why.

2. Commit to and focus on one primary goal that excites you, then write down what you want, when you want to accomplish it, and what you will give back.

3. Read your goal(s) out loud, several times a day, with enthusiasm.

4. Believe in yourself. Act on the dream now, as though it already happened. Avoid focusing on the how. Keep your mind on your dream.

FAITH

Faith is the foundation of your thoughts and emotions, the language the divine speaks and understands. When conviction has your back, you are fully supported and you can trust and surrender in gratitude, knowing that whatever you ask for is done before you utter the first word.

Faith is often difficult to have when nothing seems to have materialized in quite some time and those feelings of doubt creep in. When you doubt, you don't have confidence. When something in you just knows it will happen, it does.

Don't wonder about how things will happen; it's none of your business. Your intention is to trust your instincts and to have a steadfast belief in your desires for the highest good for all.

PRACTICE

1. Do you have faith you will receive what you desire?

2. Are you wishy-washy or doubtful? If so, stop and replace that doubt with faith.

3. Are you open to not forcing things, instead allowing them to reveal themselves?

4. Are you focused on helping others instead of only obsessing about you and your needs?

AFFIRMATIONS

Your mind is a hotbed of negativity. More than 90 percent of your thoughts are negative and are sucking away your power. That leaves 10 percent of your mind for positive thinking. We are going to change that, right now.

Affirmations are the best way to turn your negative thoughts around. Start telling yourself positive, productive, present, and helpful things rather than the depressing ideas that currently fill your head. Right now, tell yourself:

I AM LOVABLE.	I AM DESERVING.
I AM WORTHY.	I AM GORGEOUS.
I AM SAFE.	I AM WEALTHY.

Do you believe these thoughts? Or do you believe:

I AM NOT LOVABLE.	I AM NOT DESERVING.
I AM NOT WORTHY.	I AM NOT GORGEOUS.
I AM NOT SAFE.	I AM POOR.

AS YOU WISH!

Are you open to the first set of statements? If you aren't now, you will be soon. Read them again. Which do you prefer? Hopefully the first set, because if the other is more your speed, you have issues beyond my ability to help!

Embrace what you want to attract and adopt the positive thoughts and ideas that will bring about good things. Embracing struggle, negativity, and depression will only get you more of the same. Who wants that for their life? I know you don't.

What's the worst thing that could happen by focusing on positive affirmations rather than the negative? Well, you may not get your desires as quickly. Focusing on the speed with which your desires are granted is energy wasted — concentrate instead on the power of affirmations.

Many people think affirmations are a lie they tell themselves over and over. That is not even close. They are replacement thoughts, ideas that give you new programs to upload. Think of them as new lines of code that teach you to believe healthier things about yourself and your life.

Your thoughts and feelings lead to action, which creates results, right?

Your affirmations are necessary to keep your thoughts and feelings where you ideally want them to be.

Once your thoughts are empowering you, you will act differently because you are choosing to believe differently. Your results will align with what you desire rather than what you are scared or stressed about.

If you are broke right now or if your life isn't working in certain ways, you can be sure that your thoughts got you there. Your "past" thoughts were more obsessed about losing what you had or creating more of what you don't want, so you presently experience that reality. How is that working for you?

The most potent thing you can do is immediately dissolve the power of those negative thoughts and replace them with the ones that set you up to win. They are affirmations like:

You are rich. You are healthy. You are worthy. You are deserving. You can change the world. You are a generous millionaire.

PRACTICE

1. Be silent for two minutes and write down the thoughts that pop into your mind. How many are positive? How many are negative?

2. Create affirmations that support what you desire. Turn any negative thoughts into positive ones.

3. Pay attention to your thoughts and be conscious of whether or not they represent what you want for your life.

4. Record your affirmations and listen to them daily.

SPECIALIZED KNOWLEDGE

Feeling as if you can't find a logical place to start your journey only means you are lacking knowledge. You can and will be a millionaire, but not with your current mind-set or set of knowledge and thoughts. It's time to develop new understandings, new habits, and new feelings.

Think of your life up to this point as preparation for the next phase. Choose to grow, to learn, to expand — so you master your millionaire mind-set.

How will you optimize and leverage your time to make the most money doing the least amount of work? Let's say you want to make $1 million. Your current wage is $12.95 an hour and you work 40 hours per week. How long will it take you?

$1,000,000 / $12.95 / 40 / 52 = 37 years! (not including vacation days)

That's not even taking into account living expenses, taxes, or compounded interest from investments. If you saved every single penny of your income, that's how long it would take you to accumulate $1 million. Thirty-seven years.

Now let's say you're making $120 an hour and you're working 40 hours per week. How long would it take you?

$1,000,000 / $120 / 40 / 52 = 4 years! (not including expenses)

If you make $480 an hour, you will get your million in a year, not including expenses. If you aren't already a lawyer, super salesperson or doctor, how will you make that much money? That question is comprised of outdated beliefs.

If you had ten people working for you making you $50 an hour — or 20 people making you $25 an hour — you would get to be a millionaire a lot faster and easier than doing it by yourself, wouldn't you? Keep chunking it down so this millionaire idea is not overwhelming and becomes simple. Later we will go through innovative, proven ideas to achieve to this goal.

You are nothing more than a thought away from achieving your dreams.

Forget about the past and your ideas about money and work — if you don't, the restrictions will own both you and your goals. You might as well just get comfortable where you are right now because you will get stuck there.

MAKE $1 MILLION

A	B	C	D	E	F	G
NUMBER OF EMPLOYEES	PER PERSON HOURLY RATE OR HOURLY PROFIT	HOURS WORKED BY ONE PERSON PER WEEK	WEEKLY EARNINGS (A x B x C)	ANNUAL EARNINGS (52 x D)	NUMBER OF YEARS WORKED	TOTAL EARNINGS ALL YEARS (E x F)
1	$12.95	40	$518.00	$26,936.00	37.251	$1,000,002.00
1	$120.00	40	$4,800.00	$249,600.00	4.0065	$1,000,022.00
10	$50.00	40	$20,000.00	$1,040,000.00	0.9616	$1,000,064.00
20	$25.00	40	$20,000.00	$1,040,000.00	0.9616	$1,000,064.00

Table courtesy of *Actuarial and Financial Concepts*

If you think it won't happen, you are right. It won't. You need help and a team to pull off the dream. It can be done. It's done every day, all over the world, by people just like you. Read their bios, blogs, and books. Get inspired!

You can change the world, too — if you want to.

Make a difference and — who knows — maybe that goal will deliver you the opportunity to make a million...or more.

You may invent something or market a product or service that makes the world a better, cleaner place. Solar, wind, geothermal, cars running on water, algae fuel, recycling, making homes out of garbage...there are so many opportunities available to you now.

Go online, go to classes and workshops, network with those who know what you need to know, take a millionaire to lunch, interview an expert, work with someone who knows what you are missing. Hire a mentor or coach. Whatever your dream might be, act on it today.

PRACTICE

1. What don't you know about being a millionaire, loving yourself, loving others, and changing the world?

2. Are you open to new ideas?

3. Read this book, act on what you learn, do the Practice activities.

4. Go to **www.nowheretomillionaire.com**. Join the membership site so you can learn from others.

IMAGINATION

Albert Einstein once said, "Imagination is more important than knowledge."

Think of a child. Well, okay, think of one without a PlayStation or an iPod. Better yet, think of yourself as a child when an entire afternoon could be spent in a fantasy world you created with your friends or siblings. Remember being ruler of the universe? Get back to that place. Play like a child, enjoy life, and enjoy the freedom of imagination.

Imagination can change your thoughts and turn you from a negative being into a positive, happy person who doesn't have to make excuses, be defensive, always be right, or hide behind something they're not. Stop shutting down and hiding out. That's so *yesterday*.

Enjoy the comedy of life, even when it turns into a comedy of errors. Banish your fears, your doubts, and your illogical thoughts. There's nothing imaginative about that; anyone can do it.

Imagine your successful life as a heavenly dream happening right now. Experience it fully, then write down how you got what you wanted. Imagine that perfect team surrounding you, making you and them money easily.

PRACTICE

1. Have fun exploring what you want. Dream about it working out perfectly and effortlessly.

2. Imagine it's five years from now and you have succeeded. How did you do it? Who did you meet? What opportunities came your way? How did you overcome adversities?

3. See the earth as a healthy, cared-for home where you make a difference daily.

4. Imagine you and your beloved loving and being loved completely.

ORGANIZED PLAN

You cannot get where you need to be without a map. What you need is a step-by-step plan to getting what you want. If you have excavated your imagination, you already know what the experience of your dreams feels like. That will actually help you plan.

Don't be afraid to make more than one plan either. Know what works and what doesn't work — and expect the unexpected. Having a "Plan B" is never a bad idea. Think of it as your disaster-recovery plan.

Before you begin taking action, know what obstacles might arise and have alternative solutions for all of them. Mastermind with brilliant people who have the solutions before YOU come face-to-face with a challenge.

Let's face it, not every one of us is an organizational wizard. There is good news for all of you anti-OCD people out there. Plenty of people who can organize even the worst chaos with their eyes closed are available to help you. Hire that person — barter with him or her if you need to. Soon I'll show you inexpensive ways to outsource tasks with which you are weak.

If you are doing nonprofit or charitable work, people and businesses will often offer whatever you need to help others — especially when you have a plan you can share with them.

PRACTICE

1. Create a written plan to become a millionaire, change the world, and love yourself even more. There are business-plan templates available on my website.

2. Consider all the obstacles that could slow you down or stop you. Try not to be a paranoid freak, though.

3. Figure out solutions to every potential obstacle so you are resolved before you begin. Set yourself up for a win.

4. Hire others or barter so you have a team to execute your plan today.

DECISION

Decide that you are committed to the intention. Rich people decide quickly and change their mind slowly. Remember faith? You need it right now — especially if you are starting to slip back into doubt. Make a decision and stick with it. Enough second-guessing yourself; you've been traveling the circular path going nowhere for long enough.

Remember, we are going from nowhere to millionaire!

Every choice, every decision, has its pros and cons. Write them down right away to help you understand two critical points: what happens if you act now, and what happens if you keep waiting. What are the consequences of your decisions? What is the worst thing that can happen? Are you okay with that, or can you plan to solve the potential problems now?

Decide now to become a millionaire. Not just any millionaire, but one who gives back to the world while living a balanced life filled with fun, love, and possibility around every corner. Write a new story for your life.

The fable of being broke, laid off, in foreclosure, or sick is not working for you. It's a boring, old scenario and is not you. Stop telling it. Stop believing it. Act on any opportunities that are sound and well researched that take you from being a slave to an outdated, lame story to the one you desire and have faith to create.

PRACTICE

1. Decide what you want in your life now. Answer questions that inspire you to go deep, ensuring the lifestyle you want.

2. Make a decision today. Be conscious of it. Write out pros and cons so you are aware of what your choices are. Stick to what is working.

3. If you are undecided and wishy-washy, it's because you don't have faith. Commit to bolstering your faith.

4. Check your knowledge with individuals who have done what you want to do. *MAKE THE INTERNET YOUR FRIEND!*

PERSISTENCE

You will be rejected. Get used to the idea now, but don't let it get in your way or stop you. Never, ever give up. I don't care if you approach 1,000 people and each of them tells you to forget it. I don't care if you try something 10,000 times and fail each time. Keep on going!

The truth is, people who reject you because of past "failed" attempts are not what is stopping you. *You* are what is stopping you. *You* are letting fear and rejection in and listening to them as they whisper slyly in your ear, "Give up! Quit!"

You make the decision to give up or to quit, so whose responsibility do you think it is when you do?

Here's a little secret of all successful people: they set their goals, they formulate a plan, and they go for it until they get what they want. You will do that, too — as long as it is for the greatest good of all. In other words, you take care of people and the environment and are conscious of how your business today will affect seven generations in the future. Do whatever it takes to succeed and you will. Let fear take over and you won't.

This journey we are on together has no stops — for any reason. Excuses will creep their way into your head to test you. The only way to pass the test is to empty the excuses from your mind. You will find yourself far from your comfort zone — you will be pushed and prodded, and you will face seemingly difficult demands. That's when the excuses attack — and that is also when you continue to persist. You are my hero!

Find your selfless desire and forge ahead with authentic and genuine motivation.

PRACTICE

1. Practice persistence. Even when you want to stop stretching, *do it anyway*.
2. Read biographies, blogs, and books of successful people.
3. Figure out why you want to be a millionaire, to make a difference in the world, and to fall in love. **WHY** is the key word.

MASTERMIND

Surround yourself with people who believe in you and support your vision. Let them be the Presidents of your Fan Club — and you be theirs. Slam the door on those who don't support you because they suck your energy and spring leaks in your life juice. You will work too hard and get more and more stuck if you spend time hoping they will change.

Building a powerful alliance of like-minded people is the key to your success. They will be there to kick you in the butt and motivate you to keep going when you want to quit — or even just sit down for a while — because they know that if you sit too long, you won't get back up.

Know who can and will help you, who will be the best allies in the pursuit of your dream. Gather them together. Schedule regular, weekly meetings and be diligent about sticking to them.

Set a time, create an agenda, have a plan.

What are you supposed to do with all these people you've summoned to your side? Share resources, skills, and contacts. Work together to help each person bring their dreams to reality. It doesn't matter how or where you meet. It doesn't even have to be in person. Schedule a conference call if that's easier. Just meet regularly — and don't skip a meeting. No matter what, stay solution-oriented, innovative, unargumentative, and positive.

PRACTICE

1. Create a local mastermind with people you respect who are like-minded and easy to get along with.

2. Create a weekly agenda and set goals. Hold each other accountable — excuses are not allowed in this setting.

3. Go to my site and join the Community to mastermind with others: **www.nowheretomillionaire.com**.

PASSION

Passion is so attractive that people are willing to pay for it. Passion, enthusiasm, energy — can you imagine what your life would be like if you were focused on those three things? If every word, action, or feeling was founded in passion, ecstasy, and enthusiasm? Your life would be intense — and much different than it is now, I bet. You will be living in the *wow of now!*

Make passion the fuel for your life rocket.

When you are passionate, sexy, and compassionate, you exude confidence. All of this hiding out you have been doing will no longer be possible because you will be so filled with passion you'll be too busy to even find a hiding place.

Know what else will start to happen? You will create an aura of faith, desire, and determination. Others will be drawn to you and want to work with you — you won't even have to ask, you will be that incredibly desirable.

PRACTICE

1. Discover what you are **passionate** about.

2. Check in to see if you are passionate about your life. Get your *WENDY POWER* going!

3. Meet people who are excited about their life — spend time with them. Add something to their lives!

4. Find the energy within that is excited about being alive — even if, right now, that passion or excitement seems trite or unattainable. Review the steps we've gone through so far so you filter your passion using desire, faith, etc.

INTUITION

Use your guidance, your instinct, your gut, your heart, and your feelings to guide you to your dreams. Ask the divine to show you the way and trust yourself as you meet people. Look for symbols and signs to keep you directed. Listen to your inner voice.

There is an untangled expanse of inner connectedness that fills us with unity, cohesion, and an intimate communion with all that is. Experience this field, this eternal web that is connected to the heart of all things. Finding yourself by looking *out* is not the way *in*. Don't focus on outdated thoughts. The more you are aligned with stillness in spite of any apparent chaos, the more steadfast you will become as a walking, talking temple of ecstatic bliss — not needing anything outside of yourself. Your awareness will increase as easily as you breathe. You trust that you will take your next breath — there is typically no effort required, right? You are undoubting; you have faith. It's the same with intuition. Use yours to unite with the one who breathes you, the thinker behind your thoughts, the one who really sees, the wise one within who is eternal. Ask her for insight and counsel. If you are quiet and sincere, you will be reminded who you truly are. Then this game we are playing will seem effortless.

PRACTICE

1. Meet with a reputable psychic in your area and ask questions about what it means to be intuitive.

2. Read books on how to "power up" your intuition.

3. Listen to your body, your gut, your intuition. Act on what you learn.

4. Explore where you trust yourself and where you don't. Find the voice within that's wise, confident, trustworthy, and accurate.

SUBCONSCIOUS

You have a subconscious mind that works, sort of, with your conscious mind. I say "sort of" because the two have different jobs. Your conscious mind can feel, make choices, and know the difference between good and bad. Your subconscious is really just along for the ride. Think of it as a friend who follows you everywhere and is just as happy going to the city dump as they are a Broadway show.

Your subconscious mind doesn't discriminate — it simply listens to what you say and brings you what you've asked for as practically and quickly as possible. It says "Yes" to anything you think about. This is why you want to be aware of your thoughts and rigorously train them to be focused on what you want rather than what you don't want. Make sense?

Your thoughts are faster than light; you get results quickly when your subconscious and your conscious brain are aligned. Align those babies now.

PRACTICE

1. What are you feeding your subconscious? Is it nutritious?

2. What are you focused on? You'll know based on the quality of your life.

3. Identify and change anything that is not working for you. Experiment now.

OVERCOME FEAR

Fear is a little voice that comes from deep inside each of us. Fear is with you on all your adventures — but it doesn't need to stop them. Fear is founded in the past and has one primary purpose: to project doubt into the future.

Fear is False Evidence Appearing Real.

Fear is not a big, booming voice even though it might sound that way when it's speaking to you. Most likely, it's using a megaphone because fear is actually small, paranoid, and limited.

You can — and will — bring any dream to fruition faster if you ignore unfounded fear and listen to the larger, stronger, and more powerful voices that also live inside you: courage and love.

If you fear money, overcome it. *As you wish.*

If you fear change, overcome it. As you wish.

If you fear love, overcome it. *As you wish.*

Remaining stuck in the mountains of fear, worry, and doubt will not create the life of your dreams. *As you wish.*

Fear of success or failure is not real. *As you wish.*

Choose courage. *As you wish.*

PRACTICE

1. Figure out what you are afraid of and why. Is it real or imagined?

2. What has your fear cost you over the last year? Over the last five years?

3. What is or will your life be like when you are courageous?

4. Say "As you wish." Alter all your thoughts so you recognize when you are powerful and when you are fearful.

CHAPTER 5: As You Wish

"That which is looked upon by one generation at the apex of human knowledge is often considered an absurdity by the next, and that which is regarded as a superstition in one century may form the basis of science for the following one!"

— Paracelsus, 16th-century mystic and alchemist

Stop for a moment and think about your thoughts. They're nonstop, aren't they? I'm sure you sometimes wish you could slow them down or turn them off — but you simply cannot. They come and go as they please, wreak havoc as they see fit, and, on a good day, can elevate your mood and make you feel like dancing. How many do you think you have in a day? A hundred? A thousand? Nope. Try *60,000*.

Sixty-thousand thoughts in a 24-hour period. Wow!!

I just read that statistic and that's what I said — WOW! I got to thinking: *What is swimming around inside of my head 60,000 times a day?*

More important, how many are relevant, productive, and significant thoughts — and how many are mindless chatter? How many complaints, rants and trivial issues do I allow to clutter my mind tens of thousands of times a day? I don't know for sure, but I don't think I want to either. My guess is you are in the same boat.

Consider your thoughts — how many times a day do thoughts and ideas cross your mind that can birth planets, create life, change someone's life, heal someone, inspire another, or motivate you and others?

Thoughts are like a seed you plant — the question is, are you planting a weed; your favorite, fragrant flower; or nutritious food?

Think about this: how many of your thoughts are born from a small voice named Ego? Ego is a party-crasher. It finds the place where your identity, your self-confidence, and your motivation are all whooping it up and having a good time. Ego finds where they're dancing on the bar and toasting in celebration — and it barges right in, spoiling the party, offending guests, knocking over tables, and spilling drinks.

Know what makes it even worse? Ego is like the guest who won't leave.

Thoughts are a subconscious magnet — they are the greatest source of attraction, seduction, and enrollment.

Picture a fabulous genie in your mind, ready and willing to fulfill your every desire, saying "As you wish" to every thought you have. It's exciting — and it's also scary. Because sometimes you have scary thoughts. You have unhealthy, negative, depressing, and self-destructive thoughts. The genie in your head doesn't know the difference; it's trained to grant your every wish, your every desire, whether it's healthy or harmful.

Your subconscious simply says, "Yes! Yes! Yes!" to your every thought.

The universe answers back, "I'll have what she's having." Soon you give birth to your thoughts. You are about to be laid off from work. You lost your best client. You broke up with someone. You are about to enter foreclosure. You gained that ten pounds back. You produce all sorts of thoughts without even remembering what you were paying attention to in the first place.

You're like a thought slut — a thought floozy. Close your open mind and consciously choose to love those thoughts that create health, financial freedom, and unconditional love. Maybe you've used — or use — birth control? Now it's time for thought control.

I've read that computers can now "read" minds by scanning brain activity and reproducing it as video footage — as moving images of what people are seeing or remembering. You need to be your own computer, always monitoring what you are seeing or remembering. Change the channel if you aren't entertained.

When you say "I will be — I am committed to being — financially free," the powerful genie in your head responds, "As you wish."

Employing that logic, consider what would happen if you said, "I'm horrible with money. I never have any, and I'm always struggling." The same genie hears that and says, "As you wish."

Wait, what?? I didn't wish for that, what's wrong with my genie?? Nothing. She's just fine, she's doing her job to collect her paycheck while you cry about not having any money. You asked for it, you got it.

What happens next? You assume the victim role. You blame everyone but yourself. You judge the person, or persons, that you fault for your misfortune. You point your finger at circumstances. Yes, that's it! Bad luck and unfortunate circumstances — or "circus-tances" — put you in this position. No, sweetheart, they didn't. *You* put you in this position.

Accept responsibility now.

The beauty of accepting responsibility is that you are also accepting the power to change your life, yourself, and your circumstances. Why would you want to give that power to anyone else? You have spent a lifetime becoming your own person — now be that person!

I need you to make me a promise. From this point forward, after every thought you have, you will say to yourself, "As you wish." Try it now. Sit in silence for a few moments and listen to your thoughts. Do not force them, meditate if you'd like. Just pay attention to what they're saying.

Wish for something, visualize that genie in your mind, and tell her what you want. Be extravagant, be outrageous, and expand what you consider now to be "realistic." Crawl out of your head and settle comfortably into your heart. From the deepest part of your being, what is your wish? Say it out loud, then answer yourself, "As you wish." Continue to do this with every thought you have, healthy or unhealthy.

I know, I know — it sounds like a lot of extra work and extra thinking, but what you will find is a pattern. You will discover how you think, what you think — and hopefully you'll learn how to retrain your mind to filter those nasty thoughts that hold you back and smother your dreams.

Eventually, you will turn into one of Pavlov's dogs. You will be able to take off the "As you wish" shock collar because your mind will know that unhealthy thoughts equal unhealthy circumstances. It's kind of fun to be a real-life genie, isn't it?

Look around you now. Everything you see started as a thought. Thoughts are the beginning of every existence and your life is a part of that. What you have — what you live — is the love child of your thoughts. Our thoughts can be a shiny, expensive compass or a worn-out, coffee-stained road map.

What sort of life have your thoughts lived? Is it a life of vast dreams or barricading limits? Constant struggle or clear, tree-lined paths? Defensiveness or acceptance of responsibility?

The universe — or force or source of all — always answers your requests. Sometimes it just says, "No" or "Not now."

Delay isn't denial.

Sometimes other things need to appear for you to get what you want. You may need to learn more, find the right partners, develop a system, or be emotionally ready for success. Keep on your path, enjoy the travels, and don't get overattached to the results. Remember, there is supply for every demand.

Let's talk for a minute about focus. Now that you are tuned into your thoughts, what is the underlying theme? Do you spend your days worrying about what you don't have? Be careful — there's a difference between worrying about what we lack and being aware of it. An awareness of what our life does not have can be positive. Wringing your hands, pulling out your hair, burying your head in the covers, or cleaning out the carton of Ben and Jerry's is anything but positive.

Wallowing in self-pity will get you nowhere.

Unless, of course, your aim is to be sitting around in your bathrobe with 30 cats crawling around your dank apartment as you wonder, "How did I end up here?"

I'll tell you how — you let your thoughts hop into the driver's seat and take you there. Hey, you told them where you wanted to go and they said, "As you wish." Don't blame them!

That reminds me of a story about a distracted mother who was driving her daughter to school one morning when she heard her daughter scream, "Mom, you just went through a red light!"

Her mom said, "Oh, was I driving?"

Remember to always be the driver.

Esther Hicks (*The Teachings of Abraham®)* once said, "You may be saying about anything in your life: Why isn't this working for me? What am I doing wrong? What am I doing wrong? Why isn't this working for me? What am I doing wrong? What am I doing wrong? *That* is what you are doing 'wrong.'"

Stop focusing on what you *don't have* and concentrate your thoughts on what you *want* instead. Know you can — and will — have it, then have fun going out there and receiving it. Keep others in mind along your journey, do good things for them — then do even better things for them when you are a millionaire. That can be your big WHY that keeps you motivated.

Right at this moment you have a choice. You can feel powerful, confident, faithful, happy, and relaxed no matter what this bumpy road called Life has in store for you. Or you can succumb to the negative and powerless. Remember, like attracts like. The only words your genie knows are "As you wish."

Regardless of your religious or spiritual beliefs, there is one profound and secular notion to which every religious persuasion can subscribe: the universe — this greater power — wants you to have everything. The good thing about everything is that there is plenty of it! Yet, none of it will be yours if you ignore and shut out the universal energy that wants you to receive it.

You will never, ever receive any of these things if you are not open. Remember, "It is done to you as you wish." The power of the universe doesn't like closed doors. It won't waste a bit of time knocking, ringing the bell, checking to see if it's unlocked — it will simply move on until it finds a door that is open.

You, and only you, have the power to be wealthy, healthy, and in love.

"Officer, I lost my watch," says the drunk wandering around a lamppost.

"Where did you lose it?" asks the officer.

"Across the street."

"Then why are you looking for it here?"

"Because there's more light here."

Are you looking for your lost self in a place that doesn't make any sense? Sure, it might seem like the lightest, brightest, most obvious place is outside of ourselves — but the truth is, the most well-lit place is *within* ourselves. Every solution, every answer, every everything you crave and need is within you. But you will never see them if you keep shutting out introspection. Be. Do. Have. Everything you deserve.

Understand where you are, imagine where you want to be... and go there NOW.

It's responsibility time. You are now responsible for 100 percent of everything that happens in your life. You are no longer allowed to be a victim, no longer allowed to blame, no longer allowed to judge. That's been your M.O. up until now, hasn't it? What kind of life has that given you? One you've always dreamed of? I doubt it.

There was once a fabulous Wishing Tree and a gorgeous woman wished for a golden palace with solar and wind power. Poof! She instantly got it! Then she imagined her perfect soul mate. Poof! She got it! She dreamed of great riches so she could be in service to others. She manifested that easily. Then she had a thought of a monster eating her. Poof! A monster ate her.

What are you wishing for under your Wishing Tree? As you wish!

My clients always find it hard to believe that they created the foreclosure, the bankruptcy, the disease, the "bad news." They easily take responsibility for the good stuff. In fact, they don't like to share the glory and want to be recognized for their good creations. That always cracks me up. You are equally responsible for the happy stuff as well as the crappy stuff.

Mentally beating up others is your way of making yourself feel better. Blaming them and pointing fingers is truly pointing one finger at them and three at you. Think about that for a moment. Most of what we see and criticize and judge in others is a reflection of what we see and criticize and judge in ourselves. Stop that! Stop projecting your shortcomings onto other people!

Take responsibility for yourself, for your actions.
You'll like the results, trust me.

Here's another thing: you don't always have to be right. It's okay to be wrong, even though it's not much fun. Being "wrong" and admitting that you are is what helps shape you as a person. When we accept that we are not always right, we open up and listen. Maybe there is no wrong or right...maybe things aren't black and white.

You will know you have grown when you respect and value opinions that don't mirror your own. Everyone doesn't always have to agree with you and you don't have to always agree with them. Let it go. There could be truth in what you believe *and* in what someone else believes as well. At the end of the day, it doesn't matter — life goes on, the world keeps turning, and you probably won't even remember the names of the people you disagreed with. Is it really that worth it to be right? Nope.

When you have to be right, you make someone wrong. When you have to win, you make someone lose. How does that make you feel? I prefer to be happy than to be right. I like win/win scenarios. There are always at least two sides to a story, many different beliefs that are equally right, right?

Many things influence our opinions and beliefs: education, family, friends, faith, work, and the media. Your thoughts, ideas, and beliefs are actually the construct of many outside influences — very few are actually your original thoughts. That's okay, we are all programmed that way. You could be wrong because your beliefs aren't 100 percent your own. You're relying on other sources to guarantee your "rightness."

Accept that others are in the same position, and that they could have better or different sources. Or not, who knows? But does that really even matter in the grand scheme of things? Open up your mind and heart to relationships — each and everyone — because everyone in our lives has something to offer or contribute to make us a better person. You will find, I promise, that you will be a healthier, more fun, more loving, and a more open person.

Your family may actually start looking forward to holiday meals together!

It's easy to get overwhelmed with media overload and to be senseless. Taking the easy way out by letting outside influences guide your thoughts entirely is a huge waste of time. As a result, you become mindless. Mindless sucks.

Your goal is to be mindful.

Choose to be centered; open; and in a loving, balanced state of mind and heart. No more judging, no more blaming. Stop, breathe...then change.

Once you have reached this state, you have achieved success. It is from this place that miracles are born. Your acceptance is attractive to the invisible powers, the masters of things that truly matter and that deliver what you want.

You want clarity, focus, purpose, intention, and responsibility for your thoughts, feelings, beliefs, habits, actions, and results. These are your ways of human *being*. You are courageous, powerful, and passionate.

Know what you want.

Make a shopping list of what you want and take it with you everywhere as a reminder. You need a list for the grocery store or you'll forget butter — treat the list of your life desires with the same urgency.

When you're browsing the aisles at the store of life, add items that are a consuming obsession, a burning desire. Experience a definite, dominating desire to create a goal and develop a plan that is born out of faith and followed through with persistence.

We haven't even reached the best part yet. Everything I've just asked you to consider is setting you up for the most exciting part of your journey: your expedition.

What you want wants you, too!

You made out your list of what is important to you. You feel powerful, confident, and have a great sense of humor. Excellent! That's a lot farther along than you were when we started out.

Take your first baby step by committing to be rich and taking care of yourself while serving others. Nothing's better than mother's milk, don't you agree? I once saw a woman wearing an evening gown pushing a baby stroller at a park. I asked her why she was so dressed up. She said her expensive gown was the only thing that didn't smell like sour milk.

So the question is, *do a lot of your thoughts smell like sour milk?*

PRACTICE

1. Sit quietly for five minutes and notice the thoughts that come up for you. How many are negative and how many are positive?

2. Are you fighting for your limitations? What do you gain from that?

3. What has stopped you in the past?

4. Practice saying, "As you wish!" after every thought. This will allow you to realize the power of your thoughts and to witness them so you determine and consciously create your life — thought by thought.

5. Find out what you want based on what you are excited about.

6. Celebrate yourself for taking action!

CHAPTER 6: What You Want Wants You

You probably know what you want — and I'm sure you probably also know what you *don't* want.

You don't want to wake up with a raging pimple on your nose. You'd rather not have your dog French kiss you. You could do without a foreclosure notice on your front door. You would prefer that your car not break down in rush-hour traffic on the inside lane of a busy freeway. You get the idea.

When I ask clients to tell me what they don't want, their heads are immediately buried in their journals, their pens flying and faces tensing. Everyone is eager and willing to share what sucks about their lives.

When I ask them to tell me what they want, the list immediately shrinks — and it takes a great deal of thought for them to even write it in the first place. You'd think I was asking them to compose a sonnet in perfect iambic pentameter. With glazed eyes, they try to sneak glances at their neighbors' lists, wondering what they've written — or if they even have a list at all.

Every one of them wonders why this part of the exercise is so difficult. Why is their list of "don't wants" four times the size of their list of things they do?

The answer is simple: **they don't know where they are going.**

If you don't know where you are going or where you want to be, how are you going to get there? When you plan a vacation and someone excitedly asks you where you'll be spending the next week, you have an answer, don't you? Why, then, when someone asks you about the next destination for your life, do you look at them as if they've asked you for the newly revised solution to a complex calculus problem?

It's your life! You get to create it — so why aren't you?

Instead, you remain stuck in the same rut, living a small existence, staying safe, continuing to be unhappy, unfocused and doing little that you love. Take advantage of this time! Ask yourself the tough questions and don't let yourself off the hook. Get a solid understanding of what you love.

You've been waiting long enough. Your number was just called, and it's time to own up to the expectations you've put in place for your life.

Do you know what you desire? Here are some questions to ask yourself:

1. What excites me?

2. What gives me the most freedom?

3. What choice makes the greatest contribution and allows me to serve others?

4. What makes me feel the most alive, the most love, the most inner peace and happiness? What gives me the highest self-esteem?

5. What can I do to be seen or heard? How can I inspire, motivate, train, teach, coach, and activate others?

6. What is a high-profile position that pays me well, gives me time off, and lets me be a celebrity or famous person?

If you are a practical, technical person, you may instead ask:

1. What is the most practical thing for me to do now?

2. What brings me the most money with the least effort?

3. What can I outsource so others do the work while I make the money?

4. What can I systemize and organize that allows me freedom? (Get a free business plan template under "Resources" on my website and blog.)

You have come into this world to bring a certain dream to life. How can you know which dream you've come to realize? Evaluate your skills:

1. What personal skills do you have? What do others say you do well?

2. What business skills do you have?

3. What are your hobbies? What do you do for fun?

4. What do you know well? Is it exciting to you?

5. Are there skills at which you excel but do little with? Some examples are singing, art, public speaking, writing, or running a business. You have many talents and many choices!

Grab another sheet of paper and draw a line down the middle, top to bottom. On the left, list the skills you use now, personally or professionally. On the right, list the skills that are underutilized. Identify who might benefit from or be interested in them.

This exercise will help you pinpoint skills that you have and are actively using. It will also bring to light skills that you might not have right now but are open to developing. Look at the list of skills you don't currently have — these can be outsourced. We will talk more about that later in the book, but it's important that you are able to identify them now.

That's the best part of life — and of this crazy, complex world. You can always find someone to do what you don't want to do, and you can always afford their services. Bartering is a great alternative.

If you are experiencing doubt, fear, anxiety, or stress, ask yourself:

1. What do I really want for my life?

2. If this vision were alive today, what would my life be like?

3. What makes the most sense and is practical for me to follow right now?

4. What would I love to do?

5. What would I do if I knew I would succeed?

6. What would if I do if I had all the money I will ever need?

7. What is the most important thing I could create in my life right now?

What problems do you want to solve?
Are there any issues or challenges in your own home now?

I once met a woman named Rachel. She had a large family and dreaded the task of matching up orphaned socks after doing a few loads of laundry. Rachel stopped complaining and found a solution.

She created a piece of plastic that held the socks together in the wash — which meant that there was no need for a fishing expedition to find two that matched. It saved time, it was simple and it was inexpensive to produce. Now all she needed to do is promote it well and — *voilà* — a million-dollar idea.

What's your million-dollar idea? Do you have old family recipes buried deep in your kitchen cabinets that you know everyone would love? Samuel Adams beer started that way — a 100-year-old recipe handed down through the generations is now a multimillion-dollar business.

I heard about two women with less than $100 in their pockets who turned granola into a $25 million business.

I have met kids from less fortunate families who purchased their first home, as an investment, when they were 12. How'd they do it? They identified mentors, they met with them, and they used their model of success to create their own.

Mike came to the United States from Afghanistan with his family when he was just a child. A wealthy family in their home country, they were forced to flee when Russia invaded. Mike went on to learn the real estate business and live the American dream.

By the time he was 25 years old, he was worth more than $50 million.

Cordia Harrington, CEO of Tennessee Bun Company, overcame her poor and difficult background to become the woman who provides all of the buns to McDonald's. Divorced with three kids, she opened the first woman-owned McDonald's franchise — but she wasn't getting enough traffic and was struggling financially.

Did she give up? Absolutely not. She got a loan and bought into the Greyhound bus franchise, then had the buses stop near the McDonald's.

It worked. She said, "I was proud to say that 88 buses a day would stop there. That helped grow the sales a lot. In the summertime we had over 120 buses a day. Our sales rocketed to one of the top 40 in the U.S."

As if that wasn't spectacular enough, she was on the "*bun committee*" at McDonald's. As a member, she was invited to tour bakeries around the world. She soon learned that McDonald's was in need of a new bun contractor. Her baking résumé didn't even contain burnt toast, but that didn't stop her.

She spent the next four years learning everything she possibly could about the bakery business. She even sent photos of herself in a baker's cap to McDonald's executives with a caption that read: "I want to be your baker."

She was unstoppable — she had faith, a plan, specialized knowledge, imagination, desire, conviction, and the determination to do whatever it took to win that contract. She saw it in her mind over and over again, affirming that she would get the deal.

Persistence paid off. She got the contract.

She sold her franchises, invested everything she had, and then borrowed $13.5 million to start the Tennessee Bun Company business. It produces 1,000 buns a minute.

The next time you minimize your skills — be it baking cupcakes or buns, making salsa, brewing beer, or converting a hanger into a head massager — think again.

Oh, by the way, Cordia had an issue with her buns making it to market on time. What would you do if you had that problem? Do you want to guess what she did? She started a trucking company called Bun Lady Trucking...and now her buns get to market on time.

What is your biggest challenge in life? What bothers you the most about where you are or are not? Have you found the answer or the solution?

What is your million-dollar idea?

Find your dream and activate it now. Look around you. Everything started as an idea. Could you make something smaller, bigger, or easier? Could you distribute or automate it? Once you have something in your mind and heart, you will feel it and create it with all of your senses. You'll know that it is yours. Trust that you will be provided for and that what you want comes from abundance and for the good of all.

As you wish!

Live in the scene that you create. Know the outcome, in this moment. Create your future in the present.

Desire, ask, believe, receive. Don't deceive.

Live in your "imaginary" soon-to-be "real" life now. Think of all of the amazing parts of the vision and all of the potential problems or challenges you may encounter as you pursue what you want.

Think of yourself as a journalist, five years in the future, and ask yourself compelling questions about how you became a success, overcame fear, took action, and came to live such an amazing life. Do not forget that strategy — it's potent.

I developed a hypnotic audio product called *Sleep Your Way To Success*®. One of the three CDs or mp3s contains a section that presents tough questions, and the results are shocking. Everyone who listens to it takes immediate action, sees their "future" results now, and creates staggering results fast. You may want to check it out by visiting my site at **www.nowheretomillionaire.com**. Click on the "Products" tab.

Are you ready for the work it is going to take? You've seen the "future," so you know what is required of you. Write down the process, the action steps you took to attract what you desire.

PRACTICE

1. What is your million-dollar idea? We'll go over this in detail soon.

2. Imagine your life five years from now after you bring that idea to fruition. Live the success now.

When Naidine Stair was 85 years old, she wrote:

"If I had my life to live over again I would dare to make more mistakes next time. I'd relax. I would be sillier. I would take fewer things so seriously. I would laugh more. I would take more trips. I would take more chances. I would climb more mountains and swim in more rivers. I would eat more ice cream and less beans. I would have less imaginary troubles. I would ride more merry-go-rounds and pick more daisies."

What would you do if you had your life to live over? Where would you start? What would you become? What would you change? Those are tough questions I don't expect you to answer right now, but I will at the end of our journey. Here are some sweet messages to fatten your desires:

1. **You become what you think most of the time.**

   Many of us think about what we don't want so we get what we desire least. Your quality of life is determined by your thoughts — that's why it's so important to know what you're thinking about and where your obsessions lie. What are you thinking about? What do you obsess over? *As you wish!*

   Do you have tools to get you to a centered, positive place quickly; or are you focused on the negative and what you can't have?

   Discover clear, concise understandings and pictures of what you desire. Let that become your obsession.

2. **It is done to you as you believe.**

   Everything began as an idea. People surrounding the idea either really believed in it or doubted it could ever be. Those who are consistent with their beliefs, who see an idea before it physically manifests, get what they believe. They expect it to realize itself — and it does.

   What do you believe about money? About health? Love? These are the things most of us are interested in. Take time to figure out what you believe about everything. Be open to the idea that all your beliefs may be outdated, dysfunctional, small, or unhealthy. Are you open to that?

   Beliefs are thoughts you've held for a long time. Most of us are focused on thoughts from when we were five. We hold on to them, and defend them even if we are not sure if they are true anymore.

We wear these old thoughts as tight, checkered, hot pink pants that are too short with a torn blue polka-dot blouse that makes us look bloated. We make each other wrong or we use the difference as a way to create a wedge that separates us.

Just for fun, believe the opposite of what you usually believe.

If you believe that money isn't spiritual, make the decision to believe that money is very much so. If you believe that being liberal is the only way to live, spend the day looking at the world through the eyes of a conservative.

Believe the opposite of what you typically stand behind and find truth in it. There is truth in everything — but it can only be found if you are open to it. Explore what feels good to you and be tolerant of others who find pleasure in something different. Make it your ultimate goal that you will be tolerant, open, and accepting. Changes in your world ripple out and affect the whole world.

3. **You have a choice: lack or prosperity. Which do you prefer?**

Close your eyes and ask yourself, "Do I prefer to have plenty, or do I prefer to be poor?"

It's entirely up to you. *As you wish!*

You make choices that will determine the outcome of your thoughts or decisions. Love, abundance, and great health are yours if you desire them — therein lies the first step. Your thoughts and feelings lead to actions that always produce results.

Think about your life and base your assessment entirely on results. Is it working for you?

4. **Flow of good is activated by belief, faith, and acceptance. Accept Universal Good.**

If you believe — and accept — that the Universe is on your side, that it is always acting with your best interest in mind and offering lessons to be learned from the challenges you face, you will change your life instantly.

Your attitude of gratitude will soar. People will be drawn to you like a day-after-Thanksgiving sale. The truth, as I experience it, is that the flow of good is waiting to express itself as you and through you. Will you choose to be a big enough conduit?

5. **Know and trust that everything is whole and perfect, that there is a oneness underlying all thoughts, beliefs, and actions that will orchestrate your greatness. Do you choose to embrace your greatness?**

I believe there is Source — an infinite mind and heart — and that this power or force is within all of us. It is wise to listen to that part of yourself — to be, and to do from that space of oneness with Source.

If you are able, acknowledge that there is a supreme power. Some call it God; others call it Love, Gratitude, Creator, or Source. Trust that you are the one person with that energy, then ask what you desire from that one, divine energy. Be thankful. Celebrate and appreciate, trusting that what you intend is coming your way. Then, let it go. Surrender and know it is done. It will come to you faster and easier than any other way I know of.

Try it out today! It could be something like this: "I know that there is one Source called love and appreciation and I am one with that energy. I know that Universe conspires to orchestrate divine right action, people, and situations so I might easily tap into abundance and be in service to others. I feel money coming my way easily, and I'm so thankful because I know it is an answered prayer. I deserve to be wealthy and attract riches to me easily. I release this to the universe and so it is done."

Make up your own prayer that resonates for you. Avoid specifying specific amounts so as not to limit what comes your way. Be clear in your intention that it is an eternal, endless supply of wealth. We live in an abundant universe where there is plenty of everything. Get into the flow, into the electricity that is everywhere — that's the power that brings it to you and your physical world.

Many of us have made the three-dimensional matter so much we feel like the Mad Hatter. It's not the *things* we desire that serve to satisfy us, to elevate our status, to make us feel adequate, good-looking, peaceful, or happy. It is our state of grace, acceptance, selfless service, and joy in the journey that bring us ultimate satisfaction.

Sometimes during the expedition for material things and wealth, we feel a sense of loneliness as we separate from God/Source. This is why your burning purpose and desire must be aligned with what is most important to you — within your soul.

You are a matchmaker between your soul's life purpose and the heart of money.

So reunite, play, pray, and pay this divine right energy forward in everything you do. There is an overflowing abundance and opulence flowing through you if you allow it to do so.

6. There is always free will.

Attracting suffering and misery is easy. All you have to do is blame, judge, and point your finger toward someone or something else — let the world know that we don't have what we want and desire because it is everyone's and everything's fault but our own.

We blame our parents. We critique our children. We find fault in our partner. We list problems with "the system." *If only they had believed in me, if only they had supported me, if only they had said yes...then I would have what I want!*

Everyone you admire has lived any one of those stories. And you know what? At some point in their life they realized they were just stories they were making up so they didn't have to take responsibility.

Actress Hillary Swank grew up in a trailer park then later lived in a car with her mother while she was trying to make it big in Hollywood. She won the Oscar for Best Leading Actress in two movies, *Boys Don't Cry* and *Million Dollar Baby*.

I lived in my beat-up car as a teenager — and later in a single-wide in a trailer park. I know what that's like.

What is your dream? What is stopping you?

If you answered anything but *you,* you're missing the point. You *can* make it in spite of any adversity — or you won't!

As of this moment, it's time to take full responsibility for every choice you make in your life — even the ones that you wish you didn't have to experience. The violence, the anger, the abuse, the poverty, the boredom...whatever your story might be, the time to release it is now.

You are the one responsible for your life, and it's your choice whether you do it as a conscious or unconscious being. It is time to wake up; be aware, make different choices and have different preferences.

What good will come from this choice? What do you truly desire?

You must learn to love yourself fully — as you are now and as you are on this life-changing adventure. You get to stop undermining your own efforts, being resigned and cynical. This takes determination, a no-matter-what positive mental attitude, the ability to follow through with purpose, support, enthusiasm, clear vision, a goal, and a plan, right?

Remember the ladies with the buns, cupcakes, salsa, and romance novels? How about Oprah or the author of Harry Potter? If they can do it, you can do it, too!

7. The universe is infinite abundance.

There is a limitless supply of everything. You claim it, embody it, and accept it — it is whatever you can conceive. This is why you must dream big.

Do you really get that? Can you accept this belief? Can you allow it to land deeply and steep you full of the grace, appreciation, and celebration of a limitless everything? This is what is available yet so many of us resist — and what you resist persists. You want lack? You got it! How is that working for you?

You want abundance? You got it. AS YOU WISH! How is that working for you?

What do you desire? Think of some things now. Materialistic things like the car, the house, the trips, the clothes. Imagine it all. How does it feel to have those things?

If you are resisting — if you have an excuse or some negative voice that says, "I don't need those things. Those are just materialistic shallow things. People who have those things are snobby, greedy. I wasn't raised to want those things. I'm fine where I am." Blah, blah, blah. These are excuses and not real — if it's limited, it's not real.

If you are full of ideas of abundance, your nature is speaking — your divine right. It's more fun to be rich than it is to be poor. You know how you can help the poor? Don't be one of them.

8. Like attracts like.

Give and receive because we receive what we give! For everything invisible, there is a visible counterpart. You are truly a sculptor of matter and light, a great giver and receiver. Do you feel that way? *AS YOU WISH!*

You get to decide what you give before you receive. What exactly will you exchange that is of value?

Many of us have been taught not to desire anything because it leads to unhappiness.

Remember, no additional effort is required to aim high in life — to demand abundance and prosperity — than is required to accept misery and poverty.

In *Think and Grow Rich* there is a poem:

> *I bargained with Life for a penny,*
> *And Life would pay no more,*
> *However I begged at evening*
> *When I counted my scanty store.*
>
> *For Life is a just employer,*
> *She gives you what you ask,*
> *But once you have set the wages,*
> *Why, you must bear the task.*
>
> *I worked for a menial's hire,*
> *Only to learn, dismayed,*
> *That any wage I had asked of Life,*
> *Life would have willingly paid.*

So what are you asking life to pay you? What are you worth?

Many think that being rich is impossible.

Desire backed by faith knows no such word as impossible.

Every adversity brings with it the seed of an equivalent advantage, so always consider the uses of adversity.

Napoleon Hill says, "There are abundant opportunities and many dreams and needs for new, and unheard of ways to do things."

Burning desire has devious ways of transmuting itself into its physical equivalent — burning desire doesn't believe in "it can't be done" and only accepts success.

Here's what I say: dream the possible dream. Know and trust in your success. Trust that your desire wants you as much as you want it because like attracts like.

Make sure you are aligned with your passion, your heart's longing, what you cherish and consider sacred — something that serves. Tell people about your burning desire, and trust that you will succeed. It is fine if it's never been thought of because everything around you started from an idea — and many people thought the person who created it was nuts. Who cares? Do it anyway!

There is something to be said about living simply, in the present, loving life moment by moment and daring to make mistakes — just go for it! Trust yourself. Contemplate your burning desire and act upon it.

PRACTICE

1. Review the concepts and EXPERIENCE what you believe and what you don't believe.

2. Why do or don't you believe?

CHAPTER 7: Everything Popular Is Wrong

Money is energy. Most of us are willing to trade our valuable time for money. But are you filling that time, daily, with something we love passionately?

For you, I foresee the ability to accelerate your grasp on what you truly want from a grounded, courageous, steadfast focus with a "can do" attitude that is authentic and the basis for your true foundation.

You get to name your dreams and your word is law. You are intuitive, wise, compassionate, creative, graceful, nurturing, and open to receiving — because you are coming from your decisive knowing. You are a powerful being, living your life fully and responsibly.

AS YOU WISH!

In this moment, be fully satisfied, blissed, and blessed to find a business that is aligned with your core values, so you may do what matters to you.

When we typically think of getting a job or making money, we forget to ask ourselves, "What matters to me?" What's the point? To do what you love and get paid well for it! I bet you were never taught that in school, were you?

Here's a list of questions to help you decide your passion and purpose. Remember, if breasts had no nipples, they'd be pointless.

1. What do you really like to do? Write down ten of your favorites.

2. Would you do these things even if you weren't paid?

3. Do these things make you and others happy?

4. Do they serve as many people as possible?

5. Are they rewarding, fulfilling your purpose?

6. If you knew you would succeed, what would you do?

7. What does your heart long for?

8. What is sacred to you?

9. What do you care about so strongly that you can't bear to see it compromised or destroyed?

10. What do you take a stand for?

11. What would you risk everything for?

12. What do you want to bring into being?

Your inner cynic — the one who wears a coat when it's 80 degrees outside — may mumble, "Every time I think about exercise, I lie down until the thought goes away." That is the thought that ensures your life will pass you by. No pain, well, *no pain*.

Some of you will defend your tension, laziness, fear, or panic by shouting, "God put me on earth to accomplish a certain number of things. Right now I am so far behind, I will live forever!"

As they say, Time may be a healer, but often it's a lousy beautician. You need to love your inner beauty and find your purpose, point, and passion now. That means you get to answer the questions fully.

If you wait another year to do this, another year will go by. If you wait another year, another year will go by. If you wait another year, another year will go by.

If a train going 3,268 miles was heading south going 50 miles an hour and stopped for 15 minutes, how long would it take you to get there?

I have no idea.

All I know is these kinds of thoughts distract us from getting where we want to go. This is how years go by without doing what we say we want to do.

I would think that cemeteries are full of people who got distracted by things that don't matter. Every stone represents a person who dreamed of curing AIDS, feeding the hungry, writing a song. Don't let yourself be one of thousands of unmarked headstones.

Here is something that will help you know what you want.

1. **Identify what you don't want.** It's easy to do, mainly because it's what we generally obsess over. The constant focus creates the reality — we get what we don't want. We also know what we prefer and can make choices between what we want or don't want.

2. **Identify what you do want.** If you were hungry, you would probably be specific about what you want for dinner. For instance, you might say, "I love cats, they taste like chicken." Just wanted to make sure you are paying attention! Create a list of what you want in every aspect of your life: money, health, love, fun, spirituality, community, etc.

3. **Explore how you feel about what you want.** What emotions do you enjoy when you think about what you want? Do you feel love? Peace? Joy, stress, fear, or doubt? Ideally, what you want will bring feelings of pleasure, not fear. Feel them fully as you think of what you want.

4. **Spend at least 17 seconds focused on the feelings and the thoughts of attracting what you want.** If you can focus for longer, go for it. If you can't...wow! Time to practice, right? This is part of the recipe that seems to draw in the power of attraction.

5. **Expect, listen, and allow the Universe (a.k.a. Metaverse) to deliver.** Stay focused on what you want, feel the joy and the peace now as you deliberately create and attract what you desire. Let this thought and feeling become a belief. The word *belief,* according to me, means you are satisfied or comfortable with manifesting what you desire easily.

Sometimes that which we will no longer tolerate — that which causes us pain — can be the catalyst to choosing what we prefer. We are motivated both by pain and pleasure. Balance both to discover what you prefer and focus on that so you take immediate action.

Most of us seem to be more afraid to live fully than to die.

We live life thinking we are one day closer to death. If you want to knock on death's door, ring the bell and run away. It really pisses him off.

Back to the living place. This contemplation or self-inquiry is essential before we delve into the logistics of finding your business.

Your limited views of money have skewed your reality about money. What were you taught while you were growing up? *There is never enough money. Money doesn't grow on trees. We don't have enough money for that. Money is evil. People with a lot of money are snobs. Money isn't everything. Money causes suffering.*

Do any of those statements strike a painful chord? If so, I have a simple solution: send me all of your money — every cent you have — and I will gladly suffer for you. No deal, right?

Money does not cause suffering.

The only thing that causes suffering is suffering itself. You are suffering in some part of your life right now. We all are if we don't love what currently is. If I gave you $1,000, would it take away the pain? Even if your suffering is being caused by endless calls from creditors and collectors, it's likely that $1,000 would be like putting a Band-Aid on the real source of the problem.

The bottom line is this: If you are suffering without money, you will suffer with money. Before we delve any deeper into that concept, I would like you to consider four things:

1. Explore your beliefs about money. How did your parents speak to you about money when you were growing up? Do you still believe what you were taught?

2. Do you have any outdated beliefs or thoughts about being rich that are limiting or sabotaging you?

3. Are you willing now to give up those beliefs?

4. How do you truly feel about money?

Understanding your thoughts, conceptions, and ideas about wealth is important because you repeat them daily — sometimes hundreds of times — without even realizing it. In fact, you probably didn't even realize exactly what your money mind-set was until I asked you to evaluate it. Repeated thoughts become your beliefs and have led you to where you are now.

This is not a new revelation. Henry Ford once said, "If you think you can, you can. If you think you can't, you can't." Long before that, people from all walks of life said the same:

*"One's own thought is one's world. What a person thinks is
what he becomes — that is the eternal mystery."*
— Upanishads (sacred Indian scripture)

"As a man thinketh in his heart, so is he."
— Proverbs 23:7

"We are shaped by our thoughts. We become what we think..."
— Buddha

Our beliefs have become so ingrained in us that we often think they are the only way. We try to impart them — often unfairly — onto others without looking at the bigger picture. We act out, speak out, and declare our beliefs without considering who we are talking to. Let me give you an example:

A vacuum salesman appeared at the door of a woman's cottage. Without allowing the woman to speak, he rushed into the living room and threw a large bag of dirt all over her clean carpet. "If this new vacuum doesn't pick up every bit of dirt," he said, "I'll eat all the dirt."

The lady, patience lost by this time, said, "Sir, if I had enough money to buy that thing, I would have paid my electricity bill before they cut it off. Now... which would you prefer, a spoon or a knife and fork?"

Far too many of us hold on to the belief that we have to know everything.

Can you imagine Superman, seated behind a large desk covered with stacks of files, complaining to his co-workers, "The fact that I can leap tall buildings and fly faster than a speeding bullet doesn't mean I understand tax codes!"

Our beliefs — especially those about ourselves — are entrenched in pain.

These thoughts, ideas, and notions were shaped by our hurt as children — the teacher who ridiculed us, the boy or girl who broke our hearts, the boss who worked us mercilessly without a paycheck that reflected our efforts.

All of these experiences can also be remembered with pleasure, as life-changing lessons. Why do we think of ourselves as the victims instead of owning our power? Knowing that we have options, why do we focus on the ache? We maintain a belief and manipulate reality to focus on the negative. We are addicted to pain and suffering.

Why focus on limitations? Why create self-fulfilling prophecies? Why, even when it doesn't seem logical to be so rigid in our beliefs, do we unconsciously act as if they are real and look for supporting evidence so we can be right?

> *You get to figure out why you believe what you do,*
> *and what you are getting out of these beliefs.*

Understanding how you came to have such limiting beliefs is not as important as understanding why you are holding onto them. Together, we are going to choose to be self-reliant rather than the victim.

> *"Everything popular is wrong."*
> *— Oscar Wilde*

What if you did the opposite of what most people do? Conventional wisdom has pounded into our heads that we are "supposed" to go to school, get a J.O.B. (Just Over Broke), and follow the rules. Why? So we can end up in a job we hate but keep anyway since it gives us the cars, the house, and the expensive shoes? One day, you will retire and everything will fall into place and make the 40 years gone by "worth it," right?

> *No, it won't.*

Remember this statistic? *Ninety-five percent of all Americans over the age of 65 are broke.*

We're living a lot longer these days so we clearly need to do things differently. Based on results, the financial system of our childhood doesn't work. This calls for new beliefs, doesn't it?

Most of us work for our money instead of making our money work for us.

It's a new day and a new dream.

Are you following the sheeple? Are you planning to work 40-plus years grazing, glazing, dazing, rather than creating a dazzling life?

Don't be normal. It doesn't pay!

You don't want to have an out-of-money experience before your out-of-body experience begins. If you want to retire in 20 years and live on $10,000 a month, you need to enter retirement with $3.5 million.

The rules we all grew up believing in don't work if we want to retire in style. You will need new beliefs!

You can transcend anything that limits you. You don't need to defend your initial beliefs as lifelong convictions. You don't need to react to situations in the same automatic manner. Unchallenged assumptions limit your life, relationships, work, joy, and success. Does this make sense?

Instead of living unconsciously or repressing, you can bring the wounds out — quit living as a walking bruise! Discover why you maintain negative attitudes, thoughts, and beliefs.

Life can be an endless struggle full of frustrations and challenges, but eventually you'll find a hair stylist you like.

Reality is different for every one of us. We have a variety of verbal and non-verbal interpretations of everything.

Despite our differences, we all share one common limiting belief: We are not good enough.

We all repeatedly tell ourselves that there is something bad or sinful about us. As children, we often view our parents as perfect, without fault or human error. Even though we learn as adults how that belief is incorrect, we continue to spend our lives struggling to live up to their idea of perfection. We think, "If my parents are perfect. If one or both of them rejects me, there must be something wrong with me."

We carry that belief with us. As illogical as it might be, we allow our fear of rejection and abandonment to amplify the idea that there is something wrong with us. Then what do we do? We dedicate our lives to proving this belief right — or wrong — and allow it to wreak havoc on our confidence and self-esteem.

*We judge others when they are not like us or fail
to follow our rigid, outdated, and limiting beliefs.*

It's a destructive and funny circle of blame, shame, and guilt. It's a constant feeling of never being enough — and if you won't be, no one else can be enough either. We all seem to be addicted to this loop.

We aren't captivated by the dizzying circle that is making our stomach turn; we are addicted to feeling superior and smarter than everyone else. This fiction is turned into fact as we gossip, judge, and fear anyone who is different from us.

When we fear, we don't love — and there is no inner peace.

Whatever you think about someone else, you also think about yourself. Have you ever considered that? Take a second and consider a person you have found at fault — and I don't mean their inability to match their purse to their shoes. I'm talking about an inherent quality you have judged or put down. I would be willing to bet that the quality you dislike in this person is one you also reject in yourself. Do you truly believe this "fault" about yourself, or is it an automatic or unconscious belief?

Jenny Wood-Allen completed the London Marathon when she was 90, becoming the oldest woman to ever accomplish such a feat. She ran her first marathon when she was 71.

What is your excuse? What is your limiting belief?

Whatever your limiting beliefs might be, you may as well pack them all up into a big ugly cardboard box and label it one of these:

*My life was limited.
My life is limited.
My life will be limited.*

You then interpret your reality based on your beliefs. You create action based on your beliefs. Your actions create results. Results confirm your beliefs.

If you are clinging to your old beliefs, here is what you are **NOT**:

- Financially free

- In love with your body

- Feeling sexy

- Vibrantly alive

- Energetic

- Enthusiastic

- Excited

- Courageous

- Powerful

- Accepting of your mistakes

If you continually sabotage yourself, your love, your money, your health, and your relationships while simultaneously doubting yourself and judging others, blaming society and creating victim stories you are the proud owner of a whole bunch of beliefs that are the opposite of what you need to succeed.

Be honest and explore your beliefs. Ask:

1. Do you believe these statements below?

2. Where did you learn them?

3. Why do you believe them?

4. What do you get out of believing any of these statements?

5. Is the belief real?

6. Could the opposite be true?

7. Create examples of times in your life when you believed the opposite.

8. What would happen if you let go of the limiting belief? How would you feel? What actions and results would occur because you chose to believe the opposite?

Here are some typical beliefs that we are tied to:

I will never be successful.

I will always work for other people.

I have to work hard and long hours.

Work can't be fun.

My co-workers don't like me.

I don't like my body.

I'm too old to_____.

I'll never find anyone to love me.

I am unlovable.

I'm not good enough.

I'm not worthy.

I never_____.

I always _____.

I'll be blamed if I make a mistake.

I better not make a mistake.

I don't want to look foolish.

I don't deserve to be happy and wealthy.

Good things don't last.

I'm too inferior to _____.

I'm always left out.

I'm wrong.

I'm guilty.

I'm bad.

I can't trust myself.

If I'm vulnerable — I'm weak.

I'm not going to succeed.

To make a lot of money I have to deceive people.

S/he'll take care of me.

No pain, no gain.

I live within my means.

I can't spend money on myself.

I won't have enough money to retire.

My partner is wrong about how s/he spends and saves money.

I feel money is _____.

I can't be loyal to _____ and make money.

My family or church/synagogue/ mosque looks down on people with money.

I don't understand how to manage my money.

I avoid paying bills on time.

My money situation is beyond my control.

"They" keep me from getting ahead.

My investments always go down.

Money is bad.

I don't care about money.

I didn't get the right education.

It's not fair for me to have more than others.

I'm not smart enough.

What I do isn't important, so why bother.

I fail at things I try to do.

I'm right and s/he is wrong.

I win. S/he loses.

The amount of money I have determines my self-worth.

Money doesn't grow on trees.

I need to be taken care of.

Women are weaker than men.

A woman's life is harder than a man's.

Wo/men are manipulators.

I shouldn't have to work.

I'm always rejected.

I'm sick and tired of _____.

I'm poor.

Money is bad.

Money takes too much work and is stressful.

People will use me or only like me if I'm rich.

I can't do what I want.

My past dictates my present and my future.

The best part of my life is over.

It's not spiritual to have money.

People with money are greedy snobs.

My products won't sell.

I can't change my life.

I'm boring and weak.

My _____ know more than I do so I have to obey them.

I'm lazy.

The reason I can't do _____ is because _____.

The world owes me.

Take the time to consider these statements and understand your beliefs about everything. Are they helping you to feel omnipotent, prosperous, and free? If not, what *are* they doing for you?

If they are not working well for you based on what you want in your life, why hold on to them? Do you feel safer holding on to familiarity? Why?

I'll give you some reasons. You are secretly addicted to the drama. You thrive on the illusions of safety, less work, and no responsibility. You love the idea that you can be lazy, that you need not put forth effort to look good or succeed. You won't need to exercise or make friends. You can be average. No one will expect much from you. You can become what you are afraid of. You can justify your past and feel vindicated.

On the next two pages, I'd like to give you an idea of what happens to your personality based on your beliefs.

Damsel in Distress

You are dependent and needy. You rely on others to make you feel worthy and cared for, yet below the surface you feel weak, helpless, and prone to depression. You avoid responsibility and continually live a life below your capabilities because you are so focused on what you cannot do. You make others feel smothered, or you attract people who like to save others. You become their project so they remain powerful and of value to you. You may resent them for being so capable and strong or controlling.

Vixen, Temptress, Seductress

You obtain power by being desirable and may even use sex as your power play. You avoid intimacy and believe that you need to reject others before they reject you. You are looking for control and are interested only in the conquest. Your self-fulfilling prophecy leads to loneliness and a lack of intimacy and love. You may feel insecure — your conquest temporarily fulfills a shallow need.

Do Everything Right and By the Book

You need structure and order; you follow rules exactly. You feel that life has limits so you place similar limits on your thoughts and beliefs, expecting less and less. You experience your life as boring even though you may be a good employee. You may be strict, rigid, uptight, inflexible. You need to be right, and you have a sense of what is right and wrong, black and white. You may be shut down to how you feel because the rules allow you to feel less.

Pollyanna

You feel an obsessive need to "be good." As a result, you believe it's best to conform, to avoid rocking the boat. You let others dominate you or choose to only show your happy mask. You are scared to reveal your darker side — and your underlying belief is that you are not good enough. Something in you feels "bad," and you can't trust your instincts. You try harder and become a people-pleaser. You distance yourself from what you want for you. You may resent others because even as you are "supporting them," you often force yourself to hide your feelings.

Isolated Alien

Part of you may feel that the external world is untrustworthy and that people will hurt you. You avoid others and hesitate to participate much in the world. You keep your distance and don't let people in — and you are on a constant lookout for evidence to support your belief. Since you don't trust others, they tend to not trust you.

There are countless other personality types that are born from our beliefs, but these are the primary characters. You might have found that you are a mixture of two or more.

Most of our beliefs stem from the idea that we aren't good enough. We judge and label ourselves. We say over and over, "I'm a failure. I'm not good with _____. I'm a bad parent, friend, lover, etc. I'll never be enough or good with money. Everyone knows more than I do."

We respect others who also feel they aren't good enough but may hide it better than we do. We respect parents, teachers, bosses, religious leaders, doctors, "experts," the media. Forget all that. I say, "Question authority." Stop handing your power over to others, and stop paying them for their opinion about you — because they don't know any more than you do.

FIGHTING FOR YOUR LIMITATIONS

"I can't because _____." Stop labeling yourself and categorizing or compartmentalizing your life into manageable, bite-sized bits at which you do or don't excel based on past experiences.

Reevaluate statements like these:

"I can't feel good about myself because of _____."

"I can't be rich because I don't deserve or feel worthy because _____ said I'm a failure."

"I can't be rich because I'm too _____."

"I can't be rich and be loyal to _____ at the same time."

FOCUSING TOO MUCH ON YOUR PAST

Being a victim or believing that your past is also your present or your future only does one thing. It makes you a slave to your past. Your excuses will control you, and you will justify where you are now with beliefs like these:

"I can't because _____."

"I can't enjoy myself because_____."

"I've failed in the past and _____ happened."

"I tried and I can't _____."

Here is an example of how you can dissect your beliefs and get to their core:

Belief: I am poor. I am bad with money. I don't deserve money. Life is hard. Making too much money is bad. I am greedy and selfish. AS YOU WISH!

Action: Get a bad job, get laid off, make bad investments, find a partner who is also poor or not comfortable making money.

Results: Poor, foreclosure, bankruptcy, dependency, unfulfilled, sabotaging opportunities, bad investments.

Gosh, that sounds like an enriched and happy life.

JUDGING OTHERS

"Rich people are snobs. They aren't spiritual. They don't like people like me. Money is the root of all evil. I'm better than they are. Blessed are the poor and meek for they shall inherit the earth."

Justification: At least I don't have to work so much. I don't have to try too hard and have more time to _____. My parents were poor so of course I am, too. If they would have taught me, or if I went to a better school, then I would have _____.

Self-fulfilling prophecy: I'll always be poor, so why try? I'm poor because of rich people, and I don't trust them, and I don't like my boss or co-workers, so of course they don't like me.

Use WENDY POWER to explore — and possibly change — a lifelong belief.

You might find yourself saying, "I'm poor" or "I'm not successful." Can you think of a time when you had extra money or times when you were successful, even if it was modest success? How did you feel? Successful.

What were your parents' beliefs about money when you were growing up? "Money is hard work. There is never enough. You have to make millions to be considered successful." Hmmm, could that play into why you don't consider yourself successful? Now that you identified where your belief came from, can you let it go? Is it true that you need to make millions to be accomplished? If you are healthy, happy, and in love, are you successful?

Is it true that there is never enough? Is money hard work? Are there examples in your life where you found the opposite to be true? Can you turn your belief around? Money comes to me easily and is fun. There is always enough of everything. In spite of the appearance of lack, I know and trust that there is always enough.

Like attracts like. Which beliefs seem richer?
Which lead to feelings of prosperity? AS YOU WISH!

I knew someone who had endless bookcases full of labeled bottles. Without any expression or energy, she would cork and put a new bottle up on the shelf. I asked what she was doing, and she replied, "I'm bottling up my feelings."

Feel your feelings to the fullest extent possible. There is no judgment required. Feeling something versus being numb is a great place to start.

Feeling rich even when there is no physical sign
of it coming to fruition is sublime.

For years I couldn't or wouldn't cry. I felt numb or experienced some lower version of joy. I believed that sadness, rage, hurt, or frustration were unacceptable feelings. What did I do? I created a fake self. I had no idea who I really was, but I knew I was well liked because I always seemed "happy." Can you relate to the happiness mask?

Years later — post-therapy — I realized I was simply afraid of the dark side. I'd had my version of a dark night of the soul, and now I'm not afraid of it. I don't bottle up my feelings. I take time to reevaluate my beliefs based on what I prefer and what empowers me. I ask that you allow yourself to feel fully and take the time to figure out what you believe about everything that you value.

PRACTICE

1. Identify what you believe and what you value.

2. Why do you cling to it? Is it true? What do you get out of believing?

3. Exaggerate the limiting belief so it seems funny or irrational. Take it to the extreme — let go of the rigidity and experience its silliness.

4. Instead of saying, "I don't have enough money," say, "In spite of the appearance of a lack of money, I know and trust that there is plenty of money available to me — now and forever."

5. Think of times when you believed the opposite of your current belief. If you believe you don't have enough money, think of what you would do with enough money and experience the feeling you desire.

6. Imagine your limiting belief becoming a limitless belief. Sensually experience it so it seems real. How would things be different with this new, empowering conviction? How does this newly created money fulfill you and others? Be clear with your imagination so it seems real and you feel happy, safe, and prosperous.

7. Write down your old thoughts on one side of a piece of paper, then write the opposite on the other side. Identify and change your beliefs.

8. If a major idea has been controlling you, acknowledge it fully. Honor it, then bury or burn it. Grieve the thought and the time wasted defending something that has let you play too small of a game with your extraordinary life. Then let it go. Write out your new beliefs and post them where you will easily see them. Work to stop your automated reactions, and replace these old ones (your bio-computer software) with an upgrade that is less rigid and healthier.

9. Write out your new affirmations, say them often and be conscious when the old belief comes up. Acknowledge it and let it go; replace it with your new, healthier belief. Soon it will become automatic; you will see that your new belief is working better based on results.

10. Celebrate and empower your new beliefs. Acknowledge your changes one belief at a time. You will experience your life differently as you focus on what works instead of what doesn't. You will be amazed by how fast your life changes when you commit to conscious and deliberate life design. You can do this!

11. Take immediate and consistent action — using your new beliefs — to act and create new results.

CHAPTER 8:
I Will Give You $1,000

My friend Bob Allen created a billion-dollar industry with a single concept: a book and seminars on how to buy real estate with no money down. He started with a $25 classified advertisement. That one ad created a multimillion-dollar business for him.

What can you do with $25 or using the classifieds — on and offline?

Years ago he taught me something amazing, something that proves you can be a millionaire just by saving one dollar a day. Think about the day you were born and imagine your parents opening a bank account in your name with a single dollar bill. If they put in a single dollar a day into an account that made 10 percent interest, by the time you were 56 you would be a millionaire. If you earned 15 percent interest, you would be a millionaire by 40. At 20 percent interest you would have $1 million in the bank by age 32. Yes, it is that doable.

What's that I hear you thinking? It's impossible because no bank will pay 15 to 20 percent interest on your investments? Well, true...which is why you need to come up with some different strategies. Banks will use your money to make interest for themselves. Each dollar you have represents a debt. The minute you deposit it into a bank, it transforms into borrowed money — which, these days, nearly always equates to a loss.

Credit-card, mortgage, and car companies have it all figured out. They loan you money and charge compounded interest. That same dollar your loving parents put in the bank the day you were born could sit in the bank for 66 years at a 5 percent interest rate and earn you a whopping $193,000. Sure, it's nothing to sneeze at, but it's hardly a retirement cushion.

Bump that interest rate up to 10 percent and suddenly you have $2.7 million. Now we're talking. Take that dollar out of the bank and find an investment that pays 15 percent interest and suddenly you have $50 million to play with. Even better? Find something that pays 20 percent interest and at age 66 you will be sitting on $1 billion!

We are talking about $1 a day and finding something that pays interest!

If you are older, and started saving or investing later, you are obviously looking for ways to accelerate your investment. The simple answer is to save more each day. What do you waste money on now? Coffee? Cigarettes? Junk food? Alcohol? Cable TV? You bought this book because you recognize that something needs to change, right?

This is your golden opportunity.

Starting now, you are going to save daily and invest wisely. I will give you the strategy and tools to make 15, 25, and even 50 percent interest on your money with a safe, proven, government- and real-estate-backed plan.

If you save just $10 a day, it will take you 34 years at 10 percent interest, 25 years at 15 percent interest, and 20 years at 20 percent to be a millionaire. Save more, make more.

Tax liens make 12 to 50 percent interest on your money and are backed by the government. Go to my website (**www.nowheretomillionaire.com**) and look under "Wendy Recommends" to find information on tax liens. For starters, you don't need a lot of money; they are relatively safe and the learning curve is not too difficult. Imagine using this strategy to put your kids through college, put yourself through college (again or for the first time), and live a luxurious lifestyle — let your money work for you instead of letting the banks reap the rewards.

Now back to our conversation about saving money. Here are the questions you get to answer:

1. How much money do I intend to accumulate?

2. How many dollars will I save daily?

3. What interest rate will I earn on my invested dollars?

4. When will I reach my goal?

5. Why do I want this money?

Your answers may look a little like this: I will make $1 million by saving $10 a day, making 20 percent interest over 20 years so I can donate money and time to the local orphanage.

Why wait? Make a $25 donation to **www.kiva.org**. This organization creates micro-loans to individuals in developing countries. Your $25 finances a small business — and 98 percent of all loans are paid back with interest.

See how reasonable, doable, easy and specific that is? You need to commit and be consistent in your plan.

Waiting even one year costs money.

If you invest just $200 a month over 30 years at 20 percent interest and skip one year, you will have forfeited $842,803. Wow!

One year can cost you almost $1 million in future dollars. Breaking that down, you just walked away from $2,000 a day, $100 an hour. Obviously, you cannot afford to wait.

The good news? When you're down, the only place to go is up. Screw being poor. Let's become billionaires by saving $1 a day and investing it in ways that make us crazy amounts of interest.

Has the "take action now, instant gratification, gotta go do it" energy hit you? Create business cards that look like million-dollar bills and carry them with you wherever you go. Hand them out to strangers on the street and allow your subconscious to create the real thing. Remember, it doesn't know the difference between real and imaginary. I won't tell it if you don't!

My business card looks and feels like a real million-dollar bill — customized with my picture and contact info. It's so much fun! I always carry at least 20 with me. No one throws it away, and most people put it on their corkboard, computer, mirror, or in their wallet.

If you want to start feeling good about making money, and retail therapy feels like it's beyond your grasp right now, pretend to spend thousands a day.

Just imagine buying whatever you want,
wherever you want, anytime you want.

I invite you to do something different unless you are fully invested in being broke. Wait, are you? Yawn. You mean to tell me that you're not tired of that old story yet?

Get a new, crisp hundred-dollar bill and keep it in your wallet. Spend it in your mind at least 20 to 40 times a day. Buy yourself and others gifts. Donate. Buy things you need. Invest in your education. Get comfortable spending the money and knowing that there is more.

Practice feeling wealthy.

Align your feelings, thoughts, emotions, and beliefs into a prosperous consciousness. Love the abundance. Feel passionate every time you spend the money. Feel the joy, the safety, the ease and grace — and, of course, the endless gratitude and celebration.

We live in an abundant world and you deserve to
be well taken care of. Do you believe that?

The more you enjoy the experience, the more you will playfully draw it to you. Like attracts like. We live in an expansive, inclusive Universe or Metaverse. Your thoughts are expansive and include everything.

Notice when you are feeling negative and doubtful of the prosperity. Every time you do, the resistance makes it harder for what you desire to come to you. Practice faith.

Feel good — not guilty — about spending money. Know the money will become real. Experience the laws of circulation, attraction, resonance, and gratitude.

Envision yourself as a money magnet.
Money loves you. You are so attractive, you millionaire you.

You love and appreciate your wealth. If you are breathing you are rich. If you have food you are well-off. Love what you have. Appreciate what you have. If you don't enjoy what you have now — having more of what you don't appreciate will not make you happier.

Where are you now? Is your mind overtaken by the idea that you don't have enough? If so, remember this: two-thirds of the world makes less than two dollars a day, some make only one dollar a day. Feel any better? If you have running water, you are affluent and far better off than two-thirds of the WORLD'S population.

You have the ability to change your world — as well as someone else's.

I promised that if you read this book you would double your money. Remember that?

The quickest way to double your money is to fold it in half and put it back in your pocket. The other way to do it is to time-travel in your imagination. Experience yourself as a generous millionaire who uses money to be in service to others, to dream, to make a difference on the planet.

"When the soul wishes to experience something, she throws an image
of the experience out before her and enters into her own image."
— Meister Eckhart

I love that quote. It reminds me of the childhood song "Row, Row, Row Your Boat." I have found so much truth in the line, "Life is but a dream..." Dream that you can travel through time to your future. Go there, experience it, and just be. In that moment, there is no right or wrong. No one understands you when you say, "This is stupid. I have no time for this." You have the power to create anything you want through your intentions alone.

"Go confidently in the direction of your dreams!
Live the life you've imagined. As you simplify your life,
the laws of the universe will be simpler."
— Thoreau

Many clients say they can't wait to retire so they can do amazing things with their lives. That makes no sense — I tell them their programming is way off.

Why wait until the end of your life to fully enjoy it? Does that make any sense to you? It sure doesn't make sense to me, and I'm not afraid to say so.

Right now, I want you to justify why your life should be spent working 40 hours a week for 40 years, begging for two weeks off, fearful that you'll even have a job when you return because the company could go out of business — taking your 401(k) right along with it. Go ahead, I'm waiting...but I'm certainly not going to hold my breath.

I'm still here. Convince me that it's a terrific idea to live in a cubicle for 40 years instead of working when and where you want, with whomever you want. If you can sell me on that, I will give you $1,000 cash. Now, please excuse me while I go take my $1,000 and my chances to the blackjack tables — I think they're a safer bet.

Make a decision. Back it up with faith, a plan, and persistence.
Decide, right now, that it s time to enjoy your life. Finally.

Take a vacation when you want, work on the beach, make different choices, and be happy.

You have the ability to live like a millionaire even if your bank account balance is in the double digits. Before you start telling me why that's not true, here's why it is:

- Take care of someone's mansion while he or she is on vacation.

- Test-drive an exotic car today.

- Get a job on a cruise ship and travel the world.

- Become an expert and get interviewed on television or in your favorite magazine.

- Barter for services you would like. Let's say you would love to get a weekly massage and you play the guitar well enough to teach it to someone. Find a masseuse who wants to play the guitar and trade services.

- Go to the Ritz-Carlton for a drink or an appetizer. Get dressed up and meet at least three new people of influence. See if they need help with anything, and help them without asking for anything in return…for now.

- Take a millionaire to lunch, ask questions, and get coaching to fulfill your dream.

- If you want to have your own television studio, get an inexpensive high-definition camera and create a following on your YouTube channel. Make sure to have a laughing baby, a cute kitten nursing a pit pull pup, or a dog saying, "I love you" in your pitch and you are sure to be a success.

- Become a food critic for a small, local magazine, don't charge them for the reviews, and eat at the best places for free.

By the way, I did that while I was going to the Juilliard School for acting. I had very little money and was tired of peanut butter or rice and beans so I found a way to change that. I ate at the best places in New York as often as I wanted for years. It was amazing!

Do it! No excuses! I was a vegetarian and always brought a meat-eating friend to review the meat dishes. It worked out great, except when I ordered a Japanese dish and the soup came out with floating fish heads or someone's tongue.

Ask some friends to brainstorm with you on exciting ideas.

Don't focus on how you'll do it. Create the desire, the faith, the imagination, the plan, and the persistence to have a wacky, wonderful life without the excuses of being broke. Then figure out how you're going to do it.

Do the prices of hotels prevent you from traveling? Here's an idea: trade your home for someone else's. I did this recently when I traveled to San Diego over the holidays — it ended up being a trade "up" to a 10,000-square foot, 10-bedroom mansion. For two weeks I enjoyed an infinity edge pool, pool table, fantastic views…all for free. Of course, trading your home requires trust — some people might not like the idea of having a stranger in their house. I have to be honest, though, it worked great for me! If you think it would work for you, too, search online for *house swap* or *house trade.*

It's likely that some of the most fun nights of your life were those that started out with boring plans or no plans at all. You're still talking about them, aren't you? It's not the plans that make a difference. It's what you do with the situation you are given that truly matters.

Have fun and consciously design your life today. If you don t, who will?

INEXPENSIVE TRAVEL IDEAS

If you have some money and are working for yourself, and can use the internet, your phone, and a laptop, you are good to go to create awesome adventures.

RV RENTAL

You may love nature and want to see the country, but you may want to take your dog or you don't like hotels. I love RVs. They're way cool.

Search online for RV Rentals. Then call the places that rent them and ask if they need you to drive one to another location. Sometimes you'll find deals that are outrageous — instead of paying $100 a day or more, pay $20 for a top-of-the-line, fancy RV. Then take your time exploring nature in luxury!

Why would they give you a smoking great deal? It would cost them money to hire an employee to drive and pick up the RV, right? No cost to them if you do it...and they actually make a little money.

I convinced the first green RV company to lend me an amazing unit for free, for six months to a year. It even has solar panels! I support green products and inventions, so I feel great promoting their product. You can do something like this, too. Trade, barter, or give something of value in exchange so there is no money needed. Make sure you always under-promise and over-deliver!

CAR RENTAL

Try this with car rentals, too! Sometimes people drive one way and you are helping the rental car company by driving it back. Use **www.priceline.com** to pay 50 percent by bidding on the car.

AIR TRAVEL

Here are some resources to help you out and get the best prices. I love getting a deal, don't you? These sites do, too! Subscribe to e-mail lists when you find specials to where you want to go. Sometimes there are exhilarating deals to exotic places, or all-inclusive deals — meaning everything is paid for — food, drinks, activities, etc.

NOTE: These websites may not be available at the time you are reading this.

www.sidestep.com	**www.wegolo.com**
www.kayak.com	**www.cheapticketlinks.org**
www.priceline.com	**www.whichbudget.com**
www.flylc.com/directall-en.asp	**www.harefares.com**

www.bootsnall.com/internationalairfare

www.budgetlonghaul.com/index.htm

(This will give you information on long flights and cheapest prices)

TRAVEL THE WORLD

Here are inexpensive ways to travel around the world for the best price.

www.lastminuteflight.com	**www.roundtheworldticket.com**
www.mytripprice.com	**www.airtreks.com**

GET A JOB AS A TRAVEL WRITER

www.online-writing-jobs.com/jobs/freelance-travel-writing-jobs.php

www.women-on-the-road.com/travel-writing-jobs.html

VOLUNTEER TRIPS

If you are interested in volunteering and saving money as you travel the world, there are many organizations that can help. Swim with dolphins, whales or sharks; help kids; teach English; kayak; sail; hike; go on safaris and help the environment, people and animals. It's a gorgeous way to travel. Search online using the words *volunteer trips* or *volunteer vacations*.

GET A JOB ON A CRUISE SHIP
www.resourcesforyou.net

ALL-INCLUSIVE

Decide where you want to go. If you go off-season, you can travel to the Bahamas for a few hundred dollars and just pay extra for your flight. Mexico has super deals, too — you can lay on sugary-white sand with the turquoise sea for little money. Simply sell the stuff you aren't using in your closet. Have a garage sale or post items on **www.ebay.com** or **www.craigslist.org**. Suddenly, you've got yourself an all-expense-paid journey to a beachside lounge...where you can continue reading this book!

Within 72 hours, you can book a vacation — and you can even manage to do it over a weekend. Barter services and live how you'd like to in your best fantasy mind! Do it now. You deserve it.

It's easier to live like a millionaire than you thought, isn't it?

PRACTICE

1.   Do at least one exciting thing to live like a millionaire today. Even if you just have drinks at the swankiest place in your town. Test-drive a fancy car today. These ideas will cost you very little and will keep your dreams alive.

CHAPTER 9: Make Money and Outsource Your Life

Clients are always telling me that they don't know how to make extra money. That's when I ask them if they know how to speak and think. Most say, "Yes."

So now I ask you, do you know how to speak and think? If you have a brain, a mouth, a phone, and an internet connection, you can make money. If you don't know how to do something, hire someone to do it for you. Keep it simple!

Why do you want money? Some people say they want more money because they will feel more secure, peaceful, or powerful. That may or may not be true.

Here are some questions to ask yourself so you feel well cared for now while you are waiting for the money to physically manifest.

1. What can I do without the money to feel more secure, peaceful, or powerful?

   If you don't feel safe, at peace, or powerful inside, the money won't help. It will only add to your discomfort with yourself. Do more things right now that make you feel like you want to feel.

2. Why do I want what I want? Can I feel like that now? What can I do to feel those things right now?

   Do them. Get committed to achieve. Cut yourself off from any other possibility. Be of one mind.

3. What will I do to get committed to achieve my dream?

Let's explore some practical ways to make money.

If you want details on how exactly to make money using any of these strategies go to my website, **www.nowheretomillionaire.com**. Click on products and choose the ones you want to learn more about. These e-books are really inexpensive and will give you the practical steps — the exact blueprint you need to succeed.

MONEY-MAKING IDEAS

I want you to have ideas that show you how many ways there are to make a sustainable income. If you can duplicate your ideas, even better. Teach others how to do it for you and make money endlessly off of just one sale.

INVENTIONS

Instead of inventing a product, find someone with a patent who doesn't know how to market it — and sell it for them! Hire commission-only sales representatives if you are not strong in sales skills. Go to **www.uspto.gov** and find individuals with patents for things you consider interesting. Talk with them to see if you can sell, promote, or market their product.

REAL ESTATE

Instead of owning a house and selling it, find a house that is for sale at a great price then get it under contract. Where it says BUYER, write your name and the verbiage "and/or assigns." This gives you the right to resell the house to an investor and make money on the spread. You get an assignment fee — often $5,000 to over $30,000 — that is guaranteed at settlement. Each state has different rules regarding this, so make sure to research before you take action.

AFFILIATE SALES

Become an affiliate of a product. Go to **www.clickbank.com**. Find a product you want to sell — one that has a hungry, large group of buyers — and promote it. You will be given a link to track your sales and will be paid just for referring people to the product. Hire someone who is an expert at getting traffic or doing CPA (Cost Per Acquisition) deals. This means you will have a lot of people looking at the deal and won't pay until money is in your account.

JOINT VENTURES

You can become a Joint Venture Specialist! Find someone with a product they are having difficulty in marketing. Then find someone else who has a large list of people who buy similar products or services. Introduce the two parties — all while taking a 10 to 50 percent cut for your work. Start local or with vendors you are already working with — and start small so you don't feel overwhelmed. We'll go into detail on this strategy in an upcoming chapter.

INFORMATION PRODUCTS

Create an information product by recording interviews with experts who have a large following and sell the product to that market. Promote a free online class, record it using **www.freeconferencecall.com** and sell the recording in an mp3 downloadable format or as a CD that can be shipped. If you are not technical, put up an ad or hire a local student or neighborhood kid to help so the interview is recorded and burned properly. The mp3 format of downloadable audio is an awesome alternative to a compact disc because you don't have to physically ship anything and there is no artwork needed. You can sell on iTunes, **www.audible.com** or to the experts list — *and* you can create joint ventures with others who want to make money selling your interview. Make sure it's great quality information and well produced.

WRITE A BOOK

Creating a book can actually be a fairly simple process. Start by recording yourself and experts discussing a topic that interests you, then hire a transcriber at a site like **www.idictate.com**. You can then hire an editor, artist, graphic designer — a ghostwriter, if you're not a good writer — at a site like **www.elance.com.** Obtain an ISBN number then go to a self-publishing site — **www.amazon.com** is one — to sell your book. You can do a print-on-demand book at no cost until you sell one. Another alternative is an e-book, which doesn't incur any printing or shipping costs. Go to my site, **www.nowheretomillionaire.com**, to purchase e-books that provide details on most of these strategies. Another great thing about e-books? They are environmentally friendly. If you want to be a best-selling author, want to self-publish, and have $5 to $15,000 to invest, I can introduce you to an amazing team with a proven track record that can help you out.

BUY INFORMATION AND RESELL IT

If you want to get started but don't have an actual product, find countless digital products to promote at sites like **www.clickbank.com** or

www.flippa.com. People sell finished products — e-books, online videos and site memberships — often for very little money. Find a product that grabs your attention and fits your personality, one that has excellent value. Make sure there are enough people searching for that subject to ensure a built-in audience. Purchase often includes ownership — in other words, you can put your name on the book or website. Be sure you can easily forward the site to friends online via social networking sites like Twitter or Facebook. You hire a sales team with innovative ways to sell the product — that gets paid only when they get other people to look at your offer. The site takes care of payments, provides a safe and secure marketplace, and keeps track of sales, then pays you and your sales force.

SELL STUFF ON EBAY OR YAHOO STORE

What do you have of value that you don't use anymore? Sell it online, quickly and easily! Registering for an account on either site is simple and you'll find tutorials showing you exactly what to do. You'll need a digital camera and information on the product (a video is great, too!). Once you get the hang of it, you can make money from a cramped cubicle or in a beachside hammock! Drop-shipping companies allow you to purchase products for wholesale and post them for retail sale, then they ship them for you! Search the term *drop shipping*. You can get awesome prices on laptops, cameras, iPods, and all sorts of stuff people want. Do a search on eBay, for instance. Find what items most people are searching for and what they are willing to pay. Then find a drop-shipper, compare prices, get references, and check the Better Business Bureau to ensure they are legit. Soon you'll have hungry buyers ready to purchase. It can't get much easier then that, can it?

CREATE APPLICATIONS FOR SMARTPHONES AND SOCIAL NETWORKING SITES

This is a huge, ever-expanding industry and people are making a lot of money with new game, communication, and business ideas. Think of how big the market for smartphone applications is! In just two years, companies have made hundreds of millions of dollars creating games for people to download on their phones — and with mobile internet usage projected to surpass desktop usage, a mobile presence is becoming more and more essential. Use your creativity to come up with a great idea and take advantage of that need!

Work with you interests. A developer who loves to fish — and who's now a multimillionaire — created an application allowing the user to cast a line and reel in a catch by waving their phone. Another flute-loving developer created a million-dollar business by turning your phone into a woodwind instrument.

If you're not a techie, no worries. Search terms like *Facebook application developers*, *smartphone application developers*, or *iPhone iPad application developers*. This is a great way to research the process, costs, and who's out there doing it. You can post the job and gather bids for the best price at sites like **www.rentacoder.com** or **www.odesk.com**. Present your idea and get it made quickly and at great prices — ask for a quote or pay $10 to $20+ an hour for a finished product.

TAX LIENS

You can make a profit of 16 to 50 percent on tax liens. Search the term *tax liens* or go to my website at **www.nowheretomillionaire.com** and click on "Wendy Recommends" or "Products" to get more information. Most counties in the U.S. pay people to repay back taxes on properties for a great percentage return — you could end up paying pennies on the dollar for a house that's backed by the government. Check into this today! Make sure the house is not on a toxic dump site or in a neighborhood with strict homeowners association rules where you get fined for not mowing the lawn. Make sure that any system you purchase to teach you how to do this utilizes current information, as it changes often. Also be sure it's not a scam and that it gives you both the good with the bad about doing tax liens.

BARTER

Instead of paying for services, trade them! You can even get paid to arrange this for others. The Home Shopping Network (HSN) started because someone had too many can openers and sold them using the media — now it's a billion-dollar business. You can barter to get free press, free airfare, free hotel, free products, free services — it's only limited by your imagination. Search online for the word *barter* to find huge online communities that swap millions of dollars worth of services and products daily. Never make money an excuse for anything in your life!

DIRECT SALES

There are millions of amazing products that fit your passions and allow you to make money from your own sales and those of people you train. My next book will be about how to do just that — it will teach you how to research companies and compensation plans, and how to promote your product and find a qualified team to work with you. Another name for this is *network marketing* or *multilevel marketing*. There are millions of people in this business worldwide making millions upon millions of dollars in profit.

OWNING VENDING MACHINES, LAUNDROMATS, AUTOMATED CAR WASHES, BILLBOARDS, AND RV PARKS

There are countless stories about people making loads of money automatically or with very little work. Search these terms and get information on ownership with little to no money.

CREATE YOUR OWN BUSINESS

If you have a skill you've been using to make someone else a lot of money and you haven't been sharing in the profits, then it is time for you to be your own boss. You can find clients because of your skills, charge less in the beginning, or charge commission only. Outsource by hiring virtual assistants, commission-based salespeople, etc. You don't ever have to do it all alone!!!

BECOME A COACH

If you have something you can teach, or are a trainer or coach, get a high-definition video camera and record 4 to 12 video lessons demonstrating easy-to-follow step-by-step systems that are proven to work, based on results. At the end of each lesson, offer action steps as homework so your student acts on what you teach.

Your class can be 15 to 60 minutes. Remember that typical attention spans are short — if you can keep it concise, you rock! Offer only the juciest, most valuable information based on what works. Make sure your students can easily become action heros after taking your class. You need to be a passionate and enthusiastic expert, teaching based on your skills and not book knowledge.

You will create one video — to be offered free of charge — that gives potential students an overview of what the class teaches them. Tell everyone who you are, why you are qualified to teach, and what mistakes and experiences made you an expert. What system did you find or created that worked best to address problems most people have? What outcome can your students expect by taking the class? Review the benefits: "In Lesson 1 you will learn... In Lesson 2 we cover..." Give some great nuggets of secret information that entice them into purchasing access to your full-length lessons. Then say, "If you liked that, you will love my class!"

When they've signed up and go to take your class, offer a lesson that is 30 minutes or so. Show them exactly how to do what you do in a simple, easy-to-follow format. Promise that if they follow your exact steps, they will succeed.

If you need to demonstrate how to do things on a computer — editing movies or organizing your music files, for example — utilize screen recording software like Camtasia or Captivate. Presentation software like PowerPoint or even just a simple white board can also better illustrate key points or steps.

You must offer a free video, a money-back guarantee, and have a lot of passion and energy when you teach. Post your content online at **www.tingletribe.com**. It's the go to place for videos, blogs, articles, webisodes, webinars, online classes, shopping, conversation, and masterminding. You do the work once, update when necessary, and get paid forever!

And don't forget to let your talented friends know about this!

ADVERTISE YOUR WEBSITE

If you have a website that reaches 10,000 or more unique people a month, you can most likely get some ad revenue at **www.tinglenetwork.com**. Your blog or site must be insightful, well-designed and well-written. We are seeking sites that strive to be inspirational and committed to making a difference on the planet. It only take a few minutes to sign up and see if you qualify to be part of the network that reaches over 150 million people!

Let's celebrate together! Sign up now while its on your mind.

PRACTICE

1. What tasks do you dread or take too long? What tasks can you hand off to a virtual assistant?

2. What are you doing that is time-consuming and doesn't pay off?

3. If any of the ideas I wrote about sound interesting, who can you hire with the skills to help you succeed? Who knows someone who knows someone who has what you need now?

4. Commit to at least one money-making idea and then follow it through. Visit **www.nowheretomillionaire.com** and let our community know about it. You can be guided in most of these modalities with one of my coaches — simply call and set up a free coaching session today!

When I first started out in business, I felt as if my partner and I had to do everything ourselves. We couldn't afford to get help, and I was always exhausted. I want to reassure you that there are people who can help you.

A mentor of mine, Jay Abraham, asked me some interesting questions that can also help you decide what you want to be when you grow up. They will help you feel as if you're not alone, and to mastermind and work with others with whom you may have forgotten you have access.

Write down the answers — right now, before you know how we'll use them. Don't think. Just write.

PRACTICE

1. Who are the most important, powerful, respected, and influential people with whom you have a personal and direct relationship?

2. What is their power? What is their business? Over whom are they influential?

3. Who are the most specialized people you know?

4. Who, of the individuals you know, has a broader circle of contacts than yours?

5. With whom do you have indirect access?

6. With what skill sets — that are not your own — do you have access?

It's clear now how powerful you really are, isn't it? You have contacts, friends, and influencers in your immediate world who support your clear visions and goals. Now that you are thinking of who you know, it is easier to understand that there are many talented strangers who would love to support you within any budget.

There are so many ways to make money.

If you have a day job, keep it for now. If you just got laid off — congrats! Of course, you may have some reservations about moving forward. The steps you will need to take to succeed may not be those that you are good at — they may be tedious or you just may not have the expertise you need to succeed.

We typically spend too much time doing what we don't love — and that doesn't work for anyone. You get to outsource all the stuff in your life that you don't like anymore.

I find that clients often have excuses about not initiating their dreams because they say they need help, can't afford it, don't know how to find qualified people, don't have an office for them to work out of...blah, blah, blah.

You can hire people to do the things that are not your strengths.

If you don't have money right now, no worries — you can barter. What are you good at? Trade that skill for the one you need.

If you can cook or organize and someone else knows how to get traffic to your website, trade services. Don't exchange money, just exchange talents. Stop your excuses and barter today.

If you are not great at selling, marketing, or promoting yourself, find someone who is and ask them to work for you on a commission-only basis and no money out-of-pocket up front. Find interns to work for free, students who need school credits, or a referral.

This is the Tom Sawyer way to do things, right? If you have a fence to paint, find neighborhood kids to paint it for you while you do what you love.

Google *virtual assistants* and *call centers Philippines*. You'll find people who work from their home or at a call center. You can negotiate work for whatever you are willing to give, pay or trade.

Be clear on the task and set a deadline.

Here are some other cost-saving ways to find help:

- If you want a sales person, place a free listing on **www.craigslist.org** advertising the position as "commission only."

- If you need a designer, call colleges that offer academic programs specializing in what you need and offer the position to a student intern.

- If you need a secretary, hire a virtual assistant.

- If you need a transcriber, go to **www.idictate.com**.

- If you want to hire a mom at home go to **www.hiremymom.com**.

- Need people to come to your website so you can make sales? Hire a search engine optimization (SEO) expert at **www.craigslist.org** or search online for *SEO* or *PPC* (pay per click) *specialists*. They will help you get people to see your ads so you make sales.

- If you need a filmmaker, Google *demand studios* or check with the local college, or **www.craigslist.org**.

- Need a writer, editor, designer, programmer — or a multitude of other professionals? Connect and invite their bids at **www.elance.com**, **www.guru.com**, **www.odesk.com**, **www.rentacoder.com**.

- If you need to be organized go here: **www.1-2-3getorganized.com**.

- If you have extra stuff that you don't need, get rid of it. Tell yourself, "I will sell _____. I bought it and have not used it. I will sell it at a garage sale, on eBay or Craigslist today." If you don't know how to set up a store — or if you aren't the least bit technical — just find a ten-year-old to teach you.

For more resources, go to **www.nowheretomillionaire.com**.

Whatever you can think of doing, you can find someone to help you — sometimes for as little as $3 to $15 an hour. Hire individuals from the Philippines or India; consider local students in grade school, high school and even college. You are not taking advantage of anyone. Overseas, you will get college-educated, English-speaking, technical geniuses working while you sleep. *Sleep your way to success, right?*

There is always someone looking for work. They work while you relax or do what you love — and they bring in more income for you than you are paying out to them. That is the way I love to live my life...how about you?

PRACTICE

1. Think of tasks at which you do not excel, ones that take you too long to complete or are mundane. Write them down, then find interns or hire others to do the tasks.

2. Write an advertisement or listing to hire someone immediately.

3. Write out the job description, skills needed, goals, time lines, what you are willing to pay.

4. Hire the person and monitor the work. Make sure they focus on income-producing skills so they are more than paying for their time. Perhaps you want to sell extra stuff on eBay, for instance, but don't know how to do it. Hire someone who does that for a living, pay them, and make money.

5. You can get an intern to work for no pay if you have tasks that match their interest. Check local high schools and colleges.

6. Make sure you are specific and simple in your task descriptions so you don't complicate things or confuse your assistant. Let them know what you need, by when.

7. Celebrate bigtime, now!

CHAPTER 10: Grateful to Have Feet

This morning I woke up grateful that I had feet.

I curled my toes, the blue nail polish still on them, and admired their plumpness. I was mindful that these feet carry me without much complaint as I put lotion on them, delighted to watch them dance as I thought about my day.

I have a ritual about being in gratitude and giving thanks for what was, what is, and what will be based on my conscious choice. I direct my day and give it instructions as to what I intend. My day then does what it will.

There was a time when I was more invested in the outcome. I would get disappointed when the day veered off course and didn't deliver exactly what I wanted. You know what that got me? More of the same.

I used to look at myself in the mirror searching for any new hairs that had decided to emerge from my nostrils, any wrinkle of joy in need of smoothing out. I'd plump up my crow's feet because the advertisements everywhere told me that they were not attractive. Know what I mean?

We're all supposed to be the perfect trophy wives/moms/daughters/ friends/lovers, squeezed into the size-two dress and sporting the flawless makeup, golden tan, fake eyelashes, and freshly whitened teeth?

There's just one problem. The advertisers seem to have forgotten that it took me decades of laughing, smiling, and saying "I love you!" to perfectly sculpt my face. Yet, there I was — panicked and insecure — slapping on all sorts of lotion and goo onto my face because it doesn't look 18 anymore. Was worrying that I wasn't wrinkle-free going to help me be any more secure?

Can you relate to that?

If you *are* 18 right now, you've got plenty of your own issues: boy troubles, girl troubles, you can't drink, you can't go to Vegas and gamble. (Like those are really things to aspire toward.) It's likely you're dreaming of turning 21, assured that your life will suddenly be perfect.

There you are focused on your future...while the rest of us in our 30s and beyond are focusing on our past because we think that the future is scary.

We all need to breathe — and simply love what is.

Stop worrying so much about what happened five years ago — or what will happen five years from now. Find an inner peace, focus on your radiance... because you ARE radiant. Go with the flow, roll with the punches, and all those other overused clichés.

Accept what is, deal with your circumstances, live in the present, and just be excited! The opposite state of mind is absolutely draining.

I know, I know...this doesn't always work. Sometimes what "is" is not always so great. We focus on that, we obsess over it, and we let it drag us down. Regardless of what anyone else says, sometimes we would rather pull the covers up over our head and continue to feel sorry for ourselves.

I'll give you an example. Today I woke up feeling exuberant, giddy, giggly ,and full of great expectations for the day ahead. I planned that my day be something like this: make a shake, work out, walk the dogs, write while listening to sacred chants, and make a fire. Yes! A perfect day.

I knew the words would activate themselves with ease because I was filled with gratitude for being able to do what I want, when I want, where I want. I hummed a love song to myself and went downstairs.

My dogs treat me like a rock star. My boy, Casanova, howls, barks, and jumps on me with a smile. He could be telling me to buy Microsoft or maybe he's arguing the Kabbalah, it's hard to tell.

My girl, Cleopatra, does downward dog, rolls the stretch with a wag down her whole body, then walks over and gives me a great big, slobbery lick.

A welcome change from yesterday, I thought, *when they brought me a cute furry little bunny. Without a head.*

I let them out to play with two friends who stop by every morning around 6:30 to get them, watched them bound off to run over thousands of acres of land, down to the river and off to visit the neighbors for treats before returning home for breakfast. In my next life, I'm coming back as my dog.

Anyway, I went into my office after brewing some chocolate truffle vanilla chai. Much to my chagrin, there lay four piles of still-steaming, liquidy poo.

Fabulous.

I know that some of you have children, so poo means nothing to you. If we were in the same room you would be saying, "You think that's bad, yesterday the baby..." and we'd continue to top each other with horrifying stories.

Well, I don't have children, and I gag at even the smallest whiff of body odor. And now I had a big stinking pile of crap in my office.

My mind didn't love what was.

I thought about leaving it there for a while as I slipped back into bed to start my morning ritual over again.

My thoughts suddenly transformed into a metaphor that filled me with inspiration to go clean the mess up happily. Just go do it, I told myself. I don't think cleaning up crap is EVER on my list of desired daily activities, but I went out there — gagged a little bit — and cleaned things up smartly, quickly, and without all of the baggage and grumbling I have experienced in the past.

I got out my huge, heavy wet vac and the rosemary and jasmine soap. The hot water was ready, but I couldn't get the stupid cap off the compartment on the vacuum where you are supposed to put the water. I used all my strength. I used the towel and my strength. Then I used a knife and pried it open, practically shouting in my mind:

"Yes I can! I am doing this! You will not beat me!
I will do whatever it takes to open you up! You will not defeat me!
I will succeed! I am woman, hear me roar!"

I was determined and passionate. I had a burning desire and expected it to open its black plastic jaws so I could clean up the past poop.

I marched — seriously, I marched — into the smelly room and cleaned the entire carpet. My room looked new. I added a fragrance that inspires me, and I burned sage while I asked that anything stagnant and old be refreshed and blessed new.

Avoiding crap is gross. Clean it up now.

Don't avoid it or be scared of it — handle it, laugh at what used to make you grumpy, and accept your power. You're just one gag away from owning your strength.

I think we're all probably ready for a new topic.

Remember the Prince whose glorious arrival so many of you are still awaiting? You're going to be rescued? All your troubles will be left behind as you ride away in the fancy white carriage? Ring any bells?

Here's the truth: women outlive men (read: spouses) and end up in poverty.

Here's a happier truth: you can be wealthy all on your own.

I met a wonderful professional woman recently who told me about a first date with a golfer who said, "I'm gone a lot, but I'll leave you with plenty of money so you can go shopping." Needless to say, that was the last date.

As I left her office, she handed me a hot pink Post-It with a phone number of a woman who worked with Donald Trump— a woman who learned everything she needed and was now networking online with successful women to support one another's big dreams.

A woman trumping Trump. Hmmm. Interesting.

She walked me down after grabbing her knock-off designer glasses, saying, "I'll help you get the word out about *Why Marry a Millionaire? Just Be One!*" She was a top publicist for many best-selling books, so I wasn't going to turn her offer of help down.

That's what you get to do.

Say "YES!" to the support — any support.

Think of me as your perfectly fitted pink push-up bra. Let the games begin.

You don't need a man or a woman to make you wealthy, and you don't need permission to be rich. Subconsciously, you may feel you need one or both of these — don't worry, we'll take care of that. It's nothing that a little whack upside the head can't cure.

Let's start with a little love tap:

You get to do what matters to you and BE who you are — magnificent, worthy, and deserving. You will have what you desire because you say so!

Take a moment with that thought and really feel it.

You don't need someone with hairy toes to tell you that to believe it, do you?

PRACTICE

1. Know how perfect you are now. *WENDY POWER!*
2. Create your to-do list today — and do everything you write down.

FEAR IS THE FRIEND YOU TAKE ON ALL YOUR ADVENTURES

Write down your idea of a dream life. Who is with you? Where are you? What do you do? How does wealth fit into it? What do you do for fun? Involve your family, friends, environment — and don't forget to give back.

Think about all of the things you care about, what you value, and what you hold dear to your heart. It's not just about the money, so don't focus on that. Do you see how these can be integrated rather than segregated?

Imagine finances, career, relationships, community, charity, health, love, and spirituality as slices of a pie. Some are bigger than others, some are fattening and unhealthy, others are perfectly sublime taste experiences — and they're all interwoven to complete the picture of you and the world.

What we're doing together is ensuring your balance and creating an awareness that these sections are integrated. You want all the pieces to be pretty much the same. In other words, you give your attention to all the parts that make you whole. You may want to create a circle, divide it into pieces, and name them with your main focuses so you have a better idea of what is and isn't in balance.

How healthy are you and the world? The world is a mirror of our collective conscious or unconscious. Which thoughts and beliefs individually and communally work better? Choose that for yourself — be thoughtful, globally minded and aligned with your open heart. You need to be ready to make some changes that support you as a hero, a visionary, and an individual of faith with worldly values.

Imagine even more clarity and awareness as a steward of the earth. Take responsibility based on your actions. Think of whatever you do in terms of how it will affect seven generations from now.

Everything you do tells the truth about what is important to you.

Now think about where your ideas come from. Who was the thinker behind your thoughts? Did you think with your head or your heart — or both? Did you have a vision? Hear something? Have you ever thought about it before? Is this new? Are your thoughts from a new reference or an old one?

The old paradigm of a male-centric, dominating, and greedy society has not worked well, has it?

The old belief system that men are better than women, for instance, is outdated and rather ridiculous, right? I don't think any woman — if she really explores her personal beliefs, at least — believes that she is worth less than a man simply because she is a woman. Those who do have either been brainwashed or suffer from seriously low self-esteem. It's time for the divine feminine to rise, take a stand, use her power and intuition, and be a peacemaker. It's time to birth new conversations of life rather than destruction.

It's time to start taking care of future generations with each choice we make rather than grabbing for the money in spite of the consequences.

We have been seriously overusing our natural resources. In many places of the world, it is unsafe to drink the water or breathe the air. Large corporations are stealing water rights all over the world and making poor people pay for water. That is just not right.

Sex slavery is the biggest industry next to drugs. Millions of girls — some as young as four or five years old — and women are sold and trafficked to turn a profit in the sex industry. Seventy-five percent of all these girls are infected with AIDS; and are homeless, penniless, and hopeless. How are we able to close our eyes to these situations? How can we not feel a burning desire to be a solution?

You can be a mouthpiece, donating time and money. Or you can take up a cause and even lead a movement. Because you can!

You were meant to do something on the planet. There is no one like you — don't try to be someone else. You are the solution we all have been waiting for. You have the power, the understanding, the compassion, the faith, and the persistence to finally manifest whatever you desire because it's for the highest good of all.

We are stewards of the earth just as we are stewards of ourselves. Based on results, we can see that there is a great deal of introspection required so that, individually, we become the living, walking, healthy evolution of generosity.

Continuing to dig for more oil — the earth's blood — is selfish. We have proven sources of alternative energy that are clean-burning and sustainable.

Now is the time to transform yourself from reader to sacred activist.

Support only visions and businesses that prioritize green solutions. It may cost a bit more now — but that is the welcoming price of being a pioneer. There are businesses you can create that have never been thought of. There is a hungry audience with money ready to pay you generously, on time and in appreciation of your courage.

You are the one we have been waiting for.

You are being given the skills to change yourself and the world based on passion, power, prosperity, desire, focus, persistence, faith, and the change in beliefs about anything that keeps you small. There will come a time when nothing less holds your attention. You will become bored with the same, small, complaining, critical conversations mired in the illusion that this is the way things have been and therefore have to be.

You are reading this book to become who you are meant to be —
magnificent, powerful, solution-oriented, and able to meet
the right people, at the right time, for divine right action.

The money will be there. The leadership will be there. The mission and vision will be clear and powerful and rich as a metaphorical diamond (that was not mined by people who lost their life to get to it).

Say "Yes" to a life well lived. Take advantage. Dream bigger.

Do you think it's possible to attract those things you wrote out in your pie chart? Do you have any doubts or fears? What's coming up for you? What stops you from having what you desire?

Create a list of your fears now. You don't have enough time, enough money, enough self-confidence, enough information, enough certainty that you will succeed and make a difference. I've heard them all — in fact, we all have.

It's heartbreaking when people say that they don't have enough time to do what they love. In an earlier life they were talented painters, gifted musicians, or aspiring writers who gave up the dream because the need to make money took over. They walked away from their passion when the children were born.

*How do you fill in the blank? **There is an excuse for everything.***

I invite you, right now, to take on your life and do what you value. Create it from a place of courage. Let's face it, even the word *courage* can cause a tightness in the chest, can't it? I'm asking you to feel whatever is coming up for you and go for it anyway.

Go to a cemetery today. Walk around. Imagine the lives these people led. Did they do what mattered most? Let the idea of mortality seep into your bones and chill you into the recognition that *now* is the time to live fully.

PRACTICE

1. What has your fear cost you?
2. How much money?
3. How many relationships?
4. What about your health? Vibrancy? Urgency?
5. What has your fear cost you in the last five years?
6. Could fear be a child?
7. Could you love your fear?
8. Who is holding onto the fear?
9. Who is identified with the fear?

I believe that a multitude of personalities and subpersonalities live within each of us. They are holdovers from times past, here to protect, sabotage, frighten and enlighten us. You need to get in touch with them. All of them.

The critic. The child. The rebellious teen. The bully. The paranoid one. The procrastinator. The one that has a million excuses. The mean one. The funny one. The powerful one. The superhero. The emotional wreck. The damsel in distress. The slut. The one who always has to do things perfectly. The one who always has to be right. The nerd. The inner male. The inner female. The business person. The activist!

How do these personalities process fear?
What does the left brain versus the right brain think about fear?

You can even ask parts of your personality in conversation what they think about fear. You may be surprised by the answers. You may be able to overcome your doubts easier than you thought.

PRACTICE

1. Are you attached to the fear? Does it give you comfort?
2. Can you give up the ownership of fear?
3. Give up the ownership of the fear. Are you open to that?
4. Which is easier: to struggle or to be willing?
5. Which contracts you to be willing or not to be willing?
6. What do you do to avoid fear?

You may find that the one within who answers these questions is a very young you, one who remembers what happened last time or is scared to fail or succeed. Once you identify what it is for you, you can effect change.

Identify your fears. Change your identity to the fear.

We can acknowledge the fear and not tell its story. We need to meet the worry, breathe it in, and transform it with our breath so that each exhale becomes love. This is a Buddhist practice, called *TONGLEN*.

PRACTICE

1. Answer the questions and write the answers in your journal now.
2. *TONGLEN PRACTICE* — Use my process to get around fear: breathe it in fully, then exhale it as safety or love. Do that over and over again. Focus on the breath. Visualize the fear and see it transform with your breath as love.

   Imagine others experiencing this fear and, again, transform it for them. Then imagine the whole world feeling the apprehension. Now transform their trepidation with your love and your breath.

   This is a very potent practice. Transform your dread. Love your panic. Feel more compassion for the whole world, especially if you consider others to be your adversaries. Love your enemy. And don't forget to tell me about your experiences!

CHAPTER 11: Powerful Partners — Money Matchmakers

Have you ever heard the story of the Yes Men? If not, it's a pretty interesting one.

The Yes Men are an activist-duo whose unofficial mission is to raise awareness about problematic social issues. Somehow, these two guys printed 100,000 *New York Times* papers reporting only good news. They used the same logo and the same format as the *Times* publisher — people who purchased it genuinely believed it was the real paper.

Imagine that, just for a day, 100,000 people were blessed with only good news. No stories of death and destruction, no tales of hardship and woe. In its place was pure happiness and positive news.

How much time do you think is spent writing, editing, and printing the same garbage reminding everyone just how bad things are and how sad the world is? Think about the stories you wake up to each morning. People are greedy. Companies are deceptive. Money trumps human life. Thousands of people have died. A bloody war is being fought. There's an environmental disaster.

What do you think is created when your day begins with a reminder of turmoil? Nothing positive, that's for sure.

Today, try something different. Check this out: **www.nytimes-se.com**.

How great would it be to wake up and read that each day? How positive and energized and inspired did it make you feel? Tap into that inspiration.

We've all said, "I wish someone would do something about this or that." We wait for a leader to be our voice. How is that working for you? If the people start leading, the leaders will follow. Stop complaining and create a revolution! How? Become an expert!

Think of something that really drives you — something that brings you great passion — and learn as much as you can about it. Imagine that you will, one day, speak about it on live television in front of an audience of millions. Why not? Be controversial. Rock the boat. Make your statement. Change the world. You can do it with integrity. I'll teach you how.

HOW TO BECOME AN EXPERT FAST

If you have a powerful message, you just have to tell the world. Then you need to be a leading expert so people will listen to you. Find a subject that is being discussed in the media and become the go-to person on that topic. Pay attention to people who are interviewed and make notes on what you do and don't like about their presentations. Learn how to speak in passionate, articulate, do-good-for-others sound bites.

Be the good news story. Bring unique solutions to the challenges. Be courageous enough to say unpopular, controversial, make-your-hair-stand-up stuff that's not usually heard. Remember that your goal is to build a million-dollar empire! What are you passionate about? What message do you want to get out to the world? Choose a subject you want to master — *dig deep*.

PRACTICE

1. Take classes through a learning annex or local college. Attend workshops and seminars on your chosen topic.

2. Read other experts' work so you are familiar with the diverse opinions in the field of your passion. Read at least six books and all the blogs and articles you can find.

3. Interview successful individuals and find out what in their world makes people say, "Wow, I didn't know that!" Is there a solution that hasn't been addressed — and are you the one to speak about it? Test your ideas. You want people to disagree with you so you can develop the answers that get them to open their minds.

4. Use **www.freeconferencecalls.com** to record your "expert" interview. Create a product from the calls so you will have something to sell or promote. Synthesize, systemize, and sell information that has high value to others. Be sure it's excellent, comprehensive, and answers what most people want to know.

5. Join online forums and groups. Ask others what interests them most about your subject of passion and learn how to answer their questions so they are satisfied. Sell your recorded interviews to this group. You will have answered their questions and created rapport — people buy from those they like and trust.

6. Teach a free class and, in exchange, get testimonials from people attending. These provide confirmation that you are an expert.

7. Intern with the best in your field. Know your material!

8. Create a compelling press release saying you are a leading expert. People believe what they read. Write articles, even if you don't get paid. The exposure is worth it — plus your parents will be proud of you!

9. Practice your talk and rehearse answering questions. The key is to sound natural, spontaneous, and informed — and to know how to say a lot in a very short amount of time. Know what to expect before it is even asked. Create three to five tips you know will help people and give that information out freely.

10. Get a Flip or other small, inexpensive High Definition camera and record yourself, both alone and with other experts. Post the video to Facebook or YouTube. This helps gives you credibility and positions you as a leader in your subject field.

11. Use **www.prleads.com** or **www.helpareporterout.com** to find sites where producers find guests for upcoming shows.

12. Make sure to position yourself as an authority. Are you an author or founder? Do you have a rags-to-riches story or a partnership with a well-known person? Are tons of people following you on Twitter, Facebook, LinkedIn? Have you been quoted in any media coverage? Master a single focus, have a few great stories and — of course — develop three to five targeted tips.

13. Write a thank-you note to anyone who interviews you so you stand out. Arrive on time — or early — and find out as much as you can about what their audience appreciates.

Be real. Be humble. Know your material fully. Be honest about the source of your expertise. Start off with your local paper, or radio or TV station so you overcome any stuttering, shaking, or doe-in-the-headlights issues before you go on international TV. Take a class with a media expert so your presentation skills are polished. If you are well spoken, knowledgeable, and interesting, you can often get your name included in an article, news show, or magazine — plus you can help change the world! It's a blast!

HOW TO BE LIKE TOM SAWYER

I believe in the "Tom Sawyer" way of doing business. You get to have fun while someone else does the work for you.

I also believe in long-term quickie relationships. I'm not talking about a one-night stand. I'm talking about a passionate flurry of fabulously climactic activity.

In the reality you create, there is no child care needed,
no late-night calls, and no need to chauffeur anyone, anywhere.

I'm talking about something called a joint venture. You get to make money while leveraging your time, efforts, and money finding powerful partnerships.

You are the matchmaker.

Someone wants to buy, someone wants to sell — you introduce them and you get paid. Sweeeeet! You are a recession buster.

Someone wants to make more money in their business and you find the extra money by introducing them to someone with buyers for what they have. Then *you* get paid.

Seems simple enough, doesn't it? Let's explore it some more.

WHAT IS A JOINT VENTURE (JV)?

A joint venture, or JV, is how you are going to get paid the big bucks. It's about finding an opportunity to make all your dreams come true.

Work from home and work only hours that you decide.

There is, however, a small disclaimer: Not every deal will work. Not everyone will be your best friend. You will offend people. You will make mistakes. You will have some problems. You will also be making money and learning.

Talk to your fear. Kiss the monster on the nose and take immediate action. Remember to trust the process.

I learned a lot from the marketing genius of Jay Abraham and Spike Hummer. Jay is responsible for creating billions of dollars in new business through power partnerships. I spent *a lot* of money and a full year learning from them. I now know more than 95 percent of all people on the planet do about joint ventures and strategic alliances.

Now it's your responsibility to receive this information from me and take immediate action. Remember that you can outsource anything you don't like or understand.

I'm sharing these strategies and tactics with you because I want you to bring me hot, huge, money-making deals! I'll send you sensational deals as well. If you register on my website, I will e-mail you important tips and lessons about how deals are written and what to offer. I want to share valuable information with you so we can keep growing together.

First you need to *find the ones you love*. This is also known as *loverage*.

GETTING PROSPECTS

So how do you exclusively get prospects who are motivated, qualified, interested, and ready to do business with you now? When you are considering whom to work with, keep these questions in mind:

1.   What do they have or provide?

2.   What do they need or want?

3.   Who can provide the service or product that they need?

4.   What frustrates them most about business?

5.   What do they need to do to double their business this year?

Who doesn't want more money? You are the solution they have been waiting for! Your objective (at least as far as they're concerned) is to help them recession-proof their business. Business owners are always looking for more clients, revenue, and connections, right? You can approach any person in business, anywhere in the world, once you know what you're doing. You will be the bridge to more money or customers for coffee shops, artists, restaurants, car dealerships, gyms, florists, bookstores...anyone with a dream.

You will be able to approach CEOs of Fortune 500 companies and walk away with an enviable profit once you've mastered the skills and strategies I am teaching you. It's all part of our million-dollar Power Partnership strategy. If your heart just skipped a beat because that feels overwhelming, worry not.

Start small. Keep your life simple! You are a deal broker and you can do this.

Why couldn't a mechanic offer a promotion for free coffee from the next-door coffee shop while customers wait for their car repairs?

Why couldn't a gym offer a discount to the local yoga clothes shop?

Why couldn't a bookstore offer a few minutes of child care provided by a local day-care that, in return, lures their parents with a discount for after-school care?

Why couldn't a tire store offer a discount at an oil lube shop and vice versa?

Why couldn't a vampire work with a blood bank?

The possibilities are endless — and you get a percentage
of the new business — 10 to 50 percent or more!

These are simple ideas, yet you'll find that most business owners don't consider them. You explain how to do it and help them implement the exchange, then you make money. Be sure to keep it simple. Your clients could offer a coupon, a free 30-day membership for the gym, a two-for-one deal, 50 percent off with purchase...this could double their income.

There are as many ideas as there are stars — be the wish, that's all that is asked of you. Are you starting to see how exciting and seemingly obvious these things are? It's basically free for the business owner and always brings more clientele in the front door.

Someone is willing to pay you, all day long,
to come up with simple ideas that make them money.

How do you find people to JV with? Look for people with the big JV on their forehead, do an Irish step dance in clown shoes and they'll be drooling to work with you. If that doesn't work, take off your gas mask, put down the water gun, and start with people you know. You know, start with the people who already like you. People you do business with now. Think of their clients and who would be a good candidate to help them make more money.

PRACTICE

1. Don't read any more until you go through your phone book, search online for local companies that will activate your memory, and add to that wish list. Every name is a potential Ka-ching! for you both!

2. Use a spreadsheet program to compile a list of company names with phone numbers, street addresses, e-mails/websites, and types of business. This will help you keep your records organized and allows you to easily reference whose services work well together.

3. Once you do this, take a bubble bath, take the dog for a walk, or get a massage. That is an order — don't make me have to come back there!

Give yourself a lot of treats and celebrate daily.

I'm a total freak when I start a job. I absolutely cannot stop myself until it's done. This just doesn't work well in the long run because it's hard both on your body and your mind. I invite you to try what I've learned works well: working in 45-minute sessions. A timer is an awesome way to keep track of time. In these 45-minute increments, focus only on income-producing activities. You will see results from about 20 percent of your effort — it's the old 80/20 rule.

Be kind to yourself. If those terrifying, doubtful thoughts pop up, say out loud, "Thinking." That is all that is happening — you are simply thinking. Love what is and move forward. If you are in a pissy mood or have a bad case of PMS, remember that even Wonder Woman has super-lousy days. She still commits to saving the world, though, doesn't she?

You get to commit and intend daily.

What excites you? Okay, so maybe it's not making lists, calling, and asking for business or any other seemingly meaningless task, right? Wrong.

WHY?

You need your WHY, girlfriend. WHY are you committed to being a matchmaker? WHY do you want to be a recession buster, bringing money to others and making money for doing a great, exceptional, outrageous, awesome, tingly job?

If you are sincerely open to supporting others, you will succeed.

Your motivation is heart-based. Who can resist an honestly caring, passionate, inspiring, and inspired person calling because they want to work with you?

For most of us it's a dream come true. Keep your integrity and know why you get to be a millionaire. WHY? Right now you are just plain old stuck with the "I would if I could but I'm broke so I can't afford it" excuse.

That excuse truly sucks. Let's just say it so you feel it. What are you actually saying to yourself when you say you can't afford something? How does that feel? Aren't you tired of that excuse?

Start from a place of what you can afford. What can you afford? You can afford to be rich in all aspects of your life. You can afford to take a chance on yourself, right?

STEP 1: CREATE THE LIST

Commit to the one action I asked you to take and make that list of people to work with — right now. Who needs more money, business, clients, systems, and updated ways of working?

I'll give you a few more ideas for easy JVs that can make you money today — if you have a big enough WHY pushing you up your emotional hill.

- A real estate agent could offer their clients coupons at the local dry cleaners and in return she could get free dry cleaning.

- A clothing store could offer a coupon to the local jewelry store and get a percentage of any sales made with the coupon.

Now that you've got the beginning of that list together and you're smiling big and crooked as a jack-o'-lantern, it's time to write down all the companies and people you are already doing business with.

Only choose the ones you like, believe in, or are passionate about.

> Remember you are exchanging your time for money —
> make it all worth it; and value fun, integrity, and ease.

STEP 2: TWO DEGREES OF SEPARATION

Next, think about their clients. Would they be good candidates for what you're selling?

In other words, someone has an immediate challenge and they're looking for a solution — you have exactly what they want. They're happy it was that easy, they're glad to pay you, and they are thrilled to do so because they really like you and you like them.

They have a lot of friends, associates, and colleagues who have the same issue. Wouldn't they be happy to work with you and benefit from your million-dollar Power Partnership? And, of course, *they* have friends...and so it goes. Don't forget to use Facebook, Twitter, Meetup, LinkedIn, and any other social networking tools to add to your physical community.

Once you do a deal or two, remember to create a YouTube video. If you're broke, talk to any teenager and trade them something for their help. If it's your own kid...well, duh, they owe you.

I am starring in a television series with Kelly Ripa because the casting director, Andy (whom I love), saw a YouTube video of me. I was just talking (rambling, actually), without makeup (a no-no), sloppy (a no-no), drunk (kidding).

Do you see the value? Everyone uses online videos to grow businesses for free. No moolah? No excuses. If you really can't find anyone to help you do a one- to three-minute video of you speaking passionately about being a recession buster on Team Wendy, then something in you is scared and you are listening to that voice by not taking action.

Procrastinate another day.

You have the list of people you want to work with and you have figured out that you can help them find more clients, business, and money. For that, you get a healthy percentage of the extra profits you bring in.

You don't charge them a penny up front. Now you've taken away their excuses on why they can't work with you. It costs them nothing.

You can charge a small retainer to get you started; just know you may confront more resistance then if you don't charge anything up front.

In a few moments we'll go through what you say to them and how you get appointments if you don't know the business owner well. If they do know you, then we move on to...

STEP 3: THE CAMPAIGN

Let's first clarify the gist of what you are doing. You find people who trust and like you. Ask them to write a letter, send an e-mail, or make a call to their clients, offering what you are promoting, selling, or marketing. You, the deal broker, offer to split the profits.

You want to create a campaign, not just a promotion. Campaigns are finely tuned, sequenced messages that lead someone to buy after they get enough value and like you. Remember, it often takes five to eight times for someone to connect with a message and invest in you.

They do very little work and you do most of it.
They get paid well and you do, too.

The clients love it because they get a discount or a great offer for what they already want — and it's hassle-free for them. A reference from someone they trust opens a door a whole lot easier than a cold call.

Aren't you always more receptive to someone who is connected to someone you trust than you are to a perfect stranger?

If your friend (with great taste) says she loves the haircut she received at a local salon and you were looking for a new stylist to give you a fresh look, you're probably going to ask for details and contact info, right?

Say you have a friend who owns a yoga studio and you have another friend who gives phenomenal massages. Both of them keep saying they wish their business would grow. Imagine if you were able to grant them their wish and, in return, they happily gave you 25 percent of the new business that came in!

See how simple that is?

They didn't have to pay for a sales force and they don't pay you until you bring them money that they wouldn't have without you.

Maybe you are thinking of someone who has a lot of clients or a large business. What then?

STEP 4: NUTS-TO-WORK-WITH-YOU TECHNIQUES

How do you inspire people to say "Yes" to you?

Send them a container of nuts with your proposal along with a note that reads, "You'd have to be nuts not to want to make money while I do the work..."

Call them back a few days later and identify yourself as the one who sent the nuts. Believe me, they'll know who you are.

Want another trick? FedEx a handwritten letter to someone with a half of a $20 bill clipped to it and include a note that says:

"I'll give you the other half when we meet."

That will usually get you past the gatekeeper. Be sure to mark the envelope "Personal and Confidential."

That's how you get in the door. So now what? You need an appointment. Joint ventures can be developed on the phone or by e-mail — which means you can get started on the beach, from any country, or in your pajamas in a face mask eating bonbons and no one will know or care.

Say "Amen, Awomen" to that!

STEP 5: GETTING THE APPOINTMENT

Find your best smiling face. You know the one — the face that got you that special date, a promotion at work, or a fat discount on a new car. Then say, "I have a product that will greatly benefit your customers. I will do all the work and servicing, and you will be paid well without lifting a finger. I'd like to meet (or have a conference call) with you and discuss this. What's better for you, earlier or later next week?"

Then be quiet. Zip it!

Keep it simple and to the point. If they start asking questions, tell them you'll answer them all at the meeting — and remember it means they are one step closer to saying "Yes." You will be tempted to blurt out the great deal you have for them — and that's when you'll usually talk yourself out of a deal. Simply write down the time and place of the meeting...and, once again, zip it!

Then do your homework. Google the name of the individual with whom you're meeting, check them out on Facebook, Twitter, LinkedIn, MySpace, or any of the popular social networking tools. You are looking for their bio or any information on their background so you can create honest rapport and find things in common.

Knowing as much about them as possible
before your meeting is essential.

People care about what you are promoting once they know you care about them. Know their product or service, and be sure it really is a fit for what you are doing.

Check them out with the Better Business Bureau to make sure they have a good reputation. Reputation is everything — you don't want to get sucked into the sewer of success. Don't make me have to say, "I told you so."

If you start with warm leads, you'll get more "Yes" activity, though cold-calling could still result in a lot of the same, too. If it's a fit, it's a fit.

Money is seductive. Imagine if someone called you today and said, "I'll give you a lot of money and I'll do all the work."

It's kind of an irresistible offer, isn't it?

PRACTICE

1. Don't think too hard, simply take action. Check in with your local stores, the people you know, your city's Chamber of Commerce. Let them know you can bring them more money, more clients, etc.

2. Start small, so it's easy and you can make mistakes — so what, look the faster and more you "fail," the faster you will succeed. Make it a game. Celebrate the more times people say "No!" to you. You are closer to "Yes!"

3. Start with one of the simple ideas I shared with you. Don't tell them the idea until they agree to pay you a percentage of the sales. Have a simple way to keep track of the sales. If you start with people you trust, it's easier, right?

4. A simple piece of paper between you will work — I'll do this, you do that, I pay you this, by when.

5. If they ask you to design a coupon, letter, or e-mails for the campaign, worry not. Keep reading; we'll go through some of this together.

CHAPTER 12: I Think, Therefore I Am Single

The good news about joint ventures is that you'll never be single. You will mingle, tingle, and Kachingle. These techniques are great for you if you have an existing business, want to start one, or want to be a joint venture broker. You can just be starting out or be the head of a Fortune 500 company.

FULL DISCLOSURE: I am not an attorney. I didn't consult with one. I'm not an accountant. I didn't consult with one. You are on your own to check on what's best for you. Be sure to do this — it could save you many costly mistakes. In fact, follow up any credible advice by consulting with a professional. Doing so doesn't mean that you doubt the source of your advice; it just shows that you are covering all the bases and gathering as much input as possible.

That's just smart business.

If you want an attorney to check out the legality of joint ventures, an inexpensive solution can be found on my website or blog. I know of a company who — for minimal monthly fees — will review any number of contracts from anywhere in the U.S. It will be, without a doubt, one of your best investments. I have been a member for years because the benefits are well worth the money.

JVs give instant access to new clients, accelerated buy-in and trust.

They are a means to dramatically expanding your business and your client base. The best part is they either don't cost you a thing or are minimal in expense, time, and risk.

Co-branding is especially beneficial when the other company already has a great reputation. Anytime you can get your name associated with an individual or company that is well known, highly regarded, and successful — *do it.*

If you can get associated with a celebrity who is not freshly out of rehab or caught sleeping with the baby-sitter, then by all means, go for it.

Do you think the George Foreman grill would have sold as well if it was just another grill in a store? George didn't invent the thing; he simply endorsed it.

Joint ventures decrease the cost of selling, increase productivity, lower the barriers of entry, add value to clients, and are a perceived customer benefit. You can enter emerging markets immediately, and you find the resources you need without the up-front cost!

They speed up access to a lot of worldwide markets, allowing you to expand beyond your geographical boundaries.

You can be an international businesswoman in your panties and call anywhere — practically for free — using your laptop and Skype.

You can get online accessibility to sell products, send endorsed letters via e-mail, or create a video and post it on people's blogs, social networking sites, and home page — all to grow your business.

You can put inserts in magazines or with someone else's invoice. Why would someone with a product let you do that? Because they like money and they like that it doesn't take extra time. All fulfillment companies send out invoices with products; ask them to add your client's flier and share some of the profits with them — or pay to add it in the box to help them with shipping costs.

Don't make this more difficult than it has to be!

You can add your information or advertisement to newsletters or e-zines — trade something of value for the space you need in the publication.

You can get access to an already-produced infomercial and add it to sites, or buy air time at reduced rates. You only pay when someone buys the product or clicks on its link for more information.

Online ads can be inexpensive and help you to sell products or services you or your clients have. There are books and countless sites out there that can help you understand this option a bit better, but here's an overview to get you started:

Cost Per Acquisition (CPA): You are charged or make money only when someone buys the product from the ad's link. I offer recommendations for these types of ads on my website (**www.nowheretomillionaire.com**). You can also sign up for my newsletter to receive updates.

Cost Per Click (CPC): You are charged or make money when someone clicks on an ad. Yes, it's that simple.

Cost Per Lead (CPL): You get paid or are charged per lead. When someone signs up — enters their contact information — on a site, you get charged or you make money.

Cost Per Thousand (CPM): You get charged or charge money per thousand people, even if no one opens up the ad. It's not based on performance or return on investment.

P.S. — If you want to reach women online, I have great resources for you on my website and blog!

There are countless ways to make money online through advertising. In addition to the income, you will also significantly increase the traffic to your or your client's site using these techniques.

It may seem complicated at first, but it's a lot easier than wearing stilettos or preparing a dinner party for ten people. Use Google to research ad agencies so it becomes more understandable.

JVs are endorsements or referrals for clients to do business with you.

Can you see how it shortens your selling cycle, enhances sales, requires less cash, improves the lifetime value of the new client, and leaves you more time to do what you love? The cool part is it doesn't cost you anything!

You get to build your expertise. You extend your product offerings and secure your position as the leader you are. You widen the scope of your innovation and applications. You partner with products, services, or marketers — whatever you need.

If you're not up and dancing, I don't know what it's going to take!

You can share costs on advertising, research and development, selling, marketing, and clients. Here are some more ideas for you:

1. Go online. Find sites that have nonfiction books. Match them with training or coaching in that skill take 50 percent of profit on both sides to be the broker.

2. Penetrate new markets. Find people who want to sell to the same market. Share the costs incurred finding salespeople, marketing and finding clients. You get to add in your information for free.

3. Collaborate to design new products and services.

4. Get control of products or research from people who don't know how to market them.

Is your mind spinning like it did when you were a kid twirling and shouting, "Weeeee!" at the top of your lungs? Do you understand how simple this joint-venture thing can be?

It's time to come back down to earth. We've sped up the right brain, so now let's give the left brain something to do.

All you techies and systems people...it's your turn in the spotlight. Ask yourself these questions for clarity. They are not original questions, but if you take the time now to answer them — over a glass of red wine — you will be ahead of 95 percent of everyone else in business. Here we go!

Remember, this can help ANY business!

MILLION-DOLLAR QUESTIONS!

1. Who has access to what I need?

2. What do I have that others need?

3. How can I inspire salespeople to work with me?

4. How can I increase sales and profits massively?

5. Who sells to my market?

6. Who has a great reputation?

7. Who are the leaders in the market?

8. Who has access to a lot of markets worldwide?

9. How can I — quickly — expand beyond my geographical boundaries?

10. What costs can I share?

11. How can I penetrate new markets? *You can find people who want to sell or promote to the same market and let them share the cost of finding the salespeople.*

12. With whom can I collaborate to design new products or services?

13. Who will put my offer through their distribution — and vice versa?

14. Where in the world would I want to travel or have an office? What kind of bartering can I do to get free room, office, airfare, etc.?

15. Whose technology would I like to license?

16. How can I get my research and development for free?

17. How can I get control of products or research from people who don't know how to market?

18. How can I access knowledge and expertise worldwide? *This is great for specific expertise. You can convert compensation to partial ownership, sales, royalty, or the creation of your board of advisors.*

19. How can I capitalize on hidden assets, relationships, and opportunities?

20. To whom can I outsource the tasks that I am not interested in or good at?

21. How can I flip a business opportunity? *For example, you can buy a website and add some functionality or get traffic to it and resell it for more than you bought it for. Or you can assign the rights to the business or real estate and get royalties or a finder's fee for connecting buyer and seller.*

22. How can I acquire distribution, prospects, license, or borrow competencies?

23. How can I rule the world?

24. How can I repackage the business or products?

25. How can I co-brand my product or service with something that people already know and trust?

26. How can I get assets that aren't mine for little or no cost?

27. How can I stop asking so many questions?

HOW TO WORK WITH SUCCESSFUL PEOPLE

Let's say you've find someone you admire immensely. How do you break through? Send them a note, an e-mail, a special delivery, a coconut, a series of notes, a naked athlete — whatever it takes — improvising off this message:

OWNER OF AMAZING INFORMATION PRODUCT WANTS TO PUT MONEY INTO YOUR POCKET WITH NO WORK ON YOUR PART THROUGH A NO-RISK JOINT VENTURE!

Dear _____,

My name is _____ . I met you at _____ (or I met you through our mutual friend, _____.) I have a product that I believe your clients will benefit from. I'm contacting you because you are great at what you do. I'd like to work out a Joint Venture with you. You will get the biggest percentage of the sales and I will do all the work. How does that sound? Call me at _____ or e-mail me at_____.

Someone sent me this email and I found it to be really effective. Who can say no to free money if the deal is ethical, of high value at a fair price and something your clients will be interested in? Keep it simple.

So, ladies, this is when you really need to morph into Girl Dude. You've got to pretend to be packing — to have some *cajones*. Know what I mean? This is where our business conversation calls for you to reach out, to thrust, and to embrace the divine male within.

Trust your intuition — this is still a partnership we're talking about. Make sure it's a fit, full of integrity, similar values, and work ethics.

Pretend you are dating and getting married. Make sure you love each other. Remember this:

"The right half of the brain controls the left half of the body. This means that only left-handed people are in their right mind."
— Anonymous

There are at least 30 million businesses in the U.S. You can choose from any of them. More women are starting businesses than men — I think I heard it's three to one.

Offer to expand the businesses' profits beyond what they are earning now. You will get paid based on what they make or save. You work with them, offering a risk-free, performance-based opportunity.

You don't get paid unless they make or save money. You get paid 10 percent, 25 percent, or 50 percent of what you save or make them. You could ask for a retainer if you want — but this will stop some from working with you. If you're okay with that, ask for some money up front that will be paid back if you don't get them the results you promise them.

And *always* offer a risk-free guarantee — you'll get more business because they'll know you stand by your work.

Look at the next few pages for some more simple and elegant ways you can help businesses.

JOINT-VENTURE OPPORTUNITIES

1. If a seminar company only offers a low-end, introductory course, work out a deal with a company that has an advanced course or licensed material. Or go to **www.elance.com** and hire someone to create a curriculum. You do the work, they can offer input. You split it 50/50, it's a win/win.

2. Approach newsletter companies and work out a deal to make money on people who have not resubscribed. If the client/buyer renews, you get paid. This option is great if you are good on the phone or can hire people who are great closers. Offer something of value — a coupon, 2-for-1, or something for free — to anyone who chooses to renew right then and there.

3. Increase the size of any sale by adding products, upsells, cross-sells, or bonuses. You can also give them free shipping.

4. Find complementary products that past buyers may find attractive. For example, if someone purchased a spa package they may also buy a fitness program, a yoga mat, a private workout with a trainer, or massage products.

5. Show owners how to save 40 percent on overhead and take a share of it. There are many ways companies could save money from outsourcing, going to certain websites to get discounts in travel, getting tax rebates for going green, using discount media services, etc.

6. Make all ads and promotions work better. You can hire a copywriter from **www.elance.com** or **www.guru.com**. If they work in developing nations, they will charge less than most local contractors. Changing and testing one headline could make an ad work 2 to 20 times better.

7. Set up co-op deals with other companies to negotiate bigger discounts. I've done this with FedEx and UPS, ending up with a savings of 35 percent.

8. Find businesses with unique systems that work in niche markets and license it to businesses that are not as successful for $1,000 to $5,000 a year and a retainer for training. This can work well with any business. If someone is number one in

their field and making a lot of money using a proven, step-by-step system, others will pay a lot for it.

9. Look for assets that are underutilized and leverage them better. For instance, if a delivery service is only using their trucks part-time and another company can't afford to buy trucks, a win/win can be created easily by renting the trucks out as needed.

10. If one company's billing department is only used part-time, another company without a billing department can pay for the services — and you get a fee for setting up the arrangement. You could work out the deal so that you get paid as long as they do business together.

11. A lot of companies are unable to borrow money from banks. Ask them what would they do with the money if they had it now, then find companies that have what they need who are willing to trade. You get paid perpetually by both parties based on future sales. You can also trade for services you need and resell the value to yet another party.

12. You can negotiate or barter for ads, sales reps, office space, insurance, operating expenses, endorsement deals...any resource that is not being used or not filled to capacity.

14. You can help a company get better business terms, then get paid a percentage of what you save them.

15. You can buy the rights to income-generating options the business doesn't see, such as a database of inactive buyers; marketing that isn't being used but did well in the past; distributors, clients, delivery and sales forces.

16. If a retailer can't afford inventory to stock a store and has a great reputation, find another person with extra inventory, work out a consignment deal and reconsign it to the first store. Work out a deal that splits the profits in thirds between you, the store owner, and the person with the product. Test it. If the product doesn't sell, merchandise is returned without having to pay rent or salaries.

Overall, you are utilizing other people's products, services, sales force, or warehouse space. You are the middle person. You get the rights and access to the resources. You get an override from both sides without owning anything.

Set up profitable streams as fast as you want.

Get other people to do all the work so you make money while you are doing what you love. You can literally outsource *everything*. Sales reps will work on commission.

You may be great with team-building, managing, consulting, coaching, teaching, and training. If you are, I want to hear from you so we build an estrogen empire. Call your friends if anything I am saying resonates with you. Work together. Let's create a self-sustaining business that's based on the new paradigm of care, responsibility, equality, fun; and massive, passive, residual income — from home or anywhere in the world you want to work.

Many don't know how to sell their merchandise. Tie up the rights and go to markets that are hungry for the products.

There will be setbacks. Not everyone will say "Yes!" Still, you want to take action and go for it — if you don't take action and find yourself making excuses, remember what Homer Simpson says:

"Weaseling out of things is important to learn.
It's what separates us from the animals...except the weasel."

"Kids, you tried your best and you failed miserably.
The lesson is, never try."

"You don't like your job, you don't strike. You go in every day and
do it really half-assed. That's the American way."

"Oh, I'm in no condition to drive. Wait a minute...
I don't have to listen to myself. I'm drunk."

You may be tired of your excuses. It's time now to consider more ideas.

If you are a speaker and have a product or service for which you can give a lot of value as an expert, you can gain access to an organization's e-mail and client list by offering a free teleseminar — in other words, a class you teach over the phone. You can offer an agreement to split the revenue from selling your product or service — which inspires them to tell their massive list about you. I'll give you some pointers on this strategy later.

The key is to always give a lot of value, underpromise and overdeliver! Learn new things and share your message with millions!

Everyone needs profits and cash flow.
They need you and your expertise to see what they don't see.

Become a seeing eye dog. Get control of an asset, add to their business model, add new products from different fields, utilize underused assets, drive the clients to them, use their distribution network, find new ways to monetize their systems, and barter as much as you can.

You can maximize what they are doing by repurposing it in new applications. A book can become a seminar, workshop, mp3, website, eBook, video, social network site, or application for smart phones.

Find new profits and use undervalued assets.

You are the person with the plan; you have logical, exciting ways to generate new income. Businesses — if they are smart — will reward you well for bringing them money while they are hurting, trapped, and stuck.

Make sure to have everything in writing — and be clear
on what you will do and what you need them to do.

I was once told that I would make $80,000 for getting a company investment money. I brought them some solid deals after doing a lot of research. They turned down the deals, and I was not given any money for all the work I did.

It also turned out that this client's company was not a good "credit risk" to banks even though his personal credit was great. I needed to think outside my usual contacts to find a company that would loan the money he needed. I worked hard to put that together — it took *a lot* of negotiation. Rather than being grateful for the $300,000 offered to him from sources outside of the banks, he bailed on the whole deal. I didn't even get a phone call, a cup of coffee, or a hug. I learned to get a retainer and be clear that you get paid, whether they accept the deal or not. Protect yourself.

I understand why he said "No." The money wasn't cheap — but it was based on his future earnings, wouldn't be reported to his credit report, and he wouldn't be personally liable for this money.

I thought it was a great deal, considering the fact that he could borrow off this money over and over again as long as he paid back 30 percent of what he owed. It was like a never-ending line of credit based on credit-card sales.

If he had a slow month, he wouldn't owe as much money — a sweet deal, if you ask me, considering I once borrowed $200,000 for inventory and I owed the same amount every month. And my partner and I were personally liable for the money.

Please remember the lesson I learned — *be clear on your terms*. I would never again work one of these deals without a retainer that could be paid back upon completion of the loan. Don't be a sucker or be desperate for work — or worse, don't be stupid. There, yeah, I said it. *Don't be stupid.*

Make sure you have systems in place to get your money quickly.

Perform due diligence on whoever you plan to work with. Make sure they are honest — check references, check with the Better Business Bureau, check with clients. Interview the accountant and bookkeeper so you know you will be paid.

I once coached a guy's clients and got paid based on performance. It took him five months to pay me. I felt like a nag and had to find hundreds of polite ways to ask for my money since he was a friend at the time.

Make sure you are valued — and it wouldn't hurt to put something in the contract that you will add a late fee to anything not paid within ten days of the company making or saving money. This could be a daily fee, a percentage or anything that motivates the company to pay you quickly.

This business is all about leverage; you don't need a ton of money or education. You can compensate for any weakness by hiring others to do what you don't know how to do.

You can find salespeople who just work on commission.

You can get free advertising and pay only on completed sales. Performance-based advertising deals give you significant exposure for no out-of-pocket expense. When times are good, these deals are not as readily available.

You can recruit others to negotiate these deals for you and cut them in on the back end. If a sales group is selling one product or service, they can sell your product at the same time.

If you have a natural extension or up sell, many companies will welcome additional income. You work out a revenue share that is fair and you'll have a free sales team.

You can put your sales literature in packages that are shipped. This potentially saves you and the other vendor a lot of money.

In a down economy, everyone is hurting and few have a plan.

You do. It doesn't cost them money up front and it's risk-free. Now you can tap into a sales force, new distribution, advertising sources, etc.

Businesses still have to promote and market — it's their life blood. They often don't do a very good job of either, though. They are also often afraid to spend money.

That's where you come in. You share in increased profits; they don't spend any extra money. You get the option to an undervalued asset and transfer it to a more successful company. This can be inventory, database, vendors, low-cost contracts, warehouse space, past clients, equipment.... What assets can you sell quickly?

Better to sell assets than your ass!

SUSHI PLACE FOR LAWYERS CALLED "SO SUE ME"

We both know I am not an attorney — you will need to find one you can work with. I'll tell you what I've learned from interviewing a few — but remember, what they are talking about may NOT be appropriate for you. This is just to get you thinking.

Most joint ventures are created in partnership, a corporation, or Limited Liability Corporation. Ideally you want to protect your assets and not end up being personally liable for what happens in the partnership.

A corporation also offers tax advantages, which is why you would create a legal entity. You'll want to figure out ahead of time what happens if one of you wants out, wants to sell the business, dies, or gets sick. Who owns the Intellectual Property?

Now I know this is a bit of an uncomfortable way to think — everyone thinks they will live forever, that they'll be in love forever. You know that's not always the case. From day one, think the worst. You will want a Buy/Sell agreement to determine what happens if one of you wants out. Spell out who does what and who gets what percentage of the profits.

Some of you are celebrating and thinking,
"Wow, I have permission to think the worst. WAHOO!"

You want to consider *what if* because a lot of what we're talking about now relates to long-term deals. Many joint ventures are quick, in-and-out deals where you will want to have a written agreement on payment, terms, and indemnification. You don't want to get into trouble if someone is violating any copyrights, trademarks, or patents.

I'm not giving you my contracts and agreements because I am not an attorney and every state or country may have different laws. You can search for joint-venture agreements online and see what comes up, then bring it to your attorney. Make sure you have a great accountant and bookkeeper to ensure you get paid. Be certain they understand how to read your company financial records — be it a simple spreadsheet or the organized Quickbooks — to ensure you get paid fast and completely.

Sometimes you will get screwed or taken advantage of, so be smart. I once did a talk for someone and was told I would be paid for all my expenses and get a percentage of the sales. It got to the point of my having to be rude before I got reimbursed for my expenses — and I never saw a penny from sales. It happens. I truly thought this individual was trustworthy — and maybe he was. The company just didn't have the infrastructure to take care of paying me quickly.

Joint Ventures are sometimes called Affiliate Sales when they involve online deals. That is a cool way to make some serious money if you are good at getting traffic, eyeballs, or consumers to a site where they then buy what you offer. Again, you won't own the product, have to pay for inventory, insurance, overhead, employees. Go to **www.nowheretomillionaire.com** to learn about affiliate sales and how to get traffic to your offer.

THE TRUTH A NERD NEVER WANTS YOU TO FIND OUT

The two main types of joint ventures:

1. You market somebody else's stuff.

2. Somebody else helps market your stuff.

Inventors are usually nerds — I admit it, I am a nerd without the pocket protector.

Often creators think that they've got the next big thing. They will make you feel like you are so incredibly lucky to work with them and that they should get most of the money because they were dumb enough to invest tens or hundreds of thousands of dollars into something they can't sell.

They'll use the typical channels and all will reject them because they fail to see the value. This inventor will be in denial — they've got a long way to go in the grieving process. Anger and sadness will set in — won't that be a lot of fun to partner? Been there, done that. I'm telling you now, *don't do it*.

The bottom line is that if they can't sell it, they need you — and that's worth a lot of money to you. The only thing that is important is this:

Are you selling the product or not?

You are looking for people who are humble and want to work with you, who are happy to give you the bigger part of the deal because it's *found money* to them.

If people are not good to deal with in the beginning, they are not going to get easier as time goes on. Look for red flags. For example, when people are arguing with you, acting defensive, need to be right, think they know more than you do about marketing, are stubborn, have bad breath...run, don't walk, away.

> *You can easily walk away from any deal, no matter how good it seems, because there is always something better out there.*

There will also be more deals than you will be able to handle. So relax. Seriously, relax.

HOW AND WHERE DO I FIND THESE PEOPLE?

So now that your brain is spinning with the idea of working with an inventor, you're probably wondering how you connect with this person in the first place, right? Here are a few tips.

1. Attend inventors' conventions.

2. Go to **www.uspto.gov** and search through patents. You'll find tons of products with no one to market them.

3. Go to seminars or workshops that attract inventors.

4. Attend trade shows — they are full of people just starting out, as well as individuals who are already successful and open to other avenues to sell their products.

5. Join the Direct Marketing Association.

6. Take an ad out online or offline and remember to keep it simple: *"Direct marketer looking for viable direct marketing project. If you have a product you'd like to sell through direct marketing, please e-mail information to..."*

7. Go to my website and let me know you are an awesome, zippy salesperson and evangelist for products and services. I work with a lot of inventors who could use your services.

Please remember that even if you're broke, never work with people you get a bad feeling from — never! It's not worth the trouble, and it never works out. There are plenty of honest people who need what you offer — *go find them.*

TAKE THIS TIP TO HEART: Only sell something people want and are hungry for, then make sure they are buying even before you have it made. Make enough to meet the demand.

If you do it the other way around, you'll end up like me and my ex-business partner. We worked with the inventor, offered to make the product and market it — in turn, we would pay him a royalty. The product was called Toilet Trees.

Huh?

Okay, where do you hide your plunger? Well, if you bought a toilet tree, you'd hide it under a decorative plant.

Seemed like a great idea. People loved the prototype. The box had interesting toilet and environmental facts on it. The logo was a toilet with the world being flushed — the tag line read: "Don't flush the planet down the toilet." A dollar of the profits went to planting a tree in the name of the purchaser.

Cool idea, huh?! Always see where and how you can give back to organizations you care about, okay? It differentiates you from everyone else and, well, it's just the right thing to do.

Back to my story. People offered to buy them before we had it done so we thought we were going to be rich. No one bought them, not even the dollar stores, and it cost a fortune for them to sit in a warehouse. That mistake cost us $100,000. Don't make the same mistake.

Now if we had thought to partner with a toilet-plunger company or a toilet-brush company — better yet, if we had given them to real estate agents to give to clients — we might have actually sold some.

If you are sitting at home reading this and you have an idea that is expensive to produce, too big to ship easily, is being made in a country where you don't speak the language and chicken feet isn't a delicacy you can stomach — stop now. I can hear you wanting to fight with me, to defend your great idea. Shhhhh. Start small.

There are many ways to make money that don't include being a mad inventor or bringing something to market without any experience.

Yes, my partner and I were successful, usually in spite of our efforts. We had a millionaire mind-set and were focused on success, no matter what. It took a lot of juicy life and left wrinkles of time that could have been used having dinner with friends, swimming with wild dolphins, or kicking back in a backyard hammock.

Are you understanding that everything I talk to you about is to support you having a life of joy, balance, peace, and passion? Will all of it be full of laughs? Nope. That's why you outsource the stuff that stresses you and just focus on what you like.

> *Every day, do something that brings in revenue. Focus on that and your connections — networking so you're networthing.*

It's more fun to work with others than by yourself. You can leverage your time, energy, money, and have time to do what you want. Go out and meet the people now who can bring you the money, the contacts, the database, the clients, the products, and the services at a great price.

Remember, to work with me, visit **www.nowheretomillionaire.com**. I have a system set up and am looking for a few amazing people who are outgoing, honest, and can follow a system or make it better.

DISTRIBUTORSHIPS

With a distributorship, you get the right to distribute someone's product and often won't get an exclusive. It's a simple arrangement. Find out what territories are available and try to get an exclusive in an area. You are basically saying, "Here is my product. Now go out and sell it." Sometimes they require that you buy a certain number of items to qualify for a discounted price.

If you are looking for distributors, keep the deal non-exclusive. Ideally, you'll want to set a minimum for sales if you do an exclusive region.

CONSULTING ARRANGEMENTS

If you have the right skills, you can get paid as a consultant — providing services like marketing, sales, copywriting, or advertising. You charge a fee and a percentage or royalty, acting as an independent contractor. It is usually best to charge a fee to avoid not getting paid for your hard work.

You can charge a fee, a retainer, or royalties and you can negotiate a piece of ownership — or equity — in the client's company.

If you are writing for someone as part of a deal, negotiate the copyright. Will you own it or will they own it by making you a *work-for-hire?* This means they own whatever you write for them.

There are so many ideas out there that can help you find out what you need to succeed.

You can speak at events and arrange a 50/50 split of product sales with the promoter.

You can get your product on TV, radio, and print by doing a per-inquiry deal — you won't pay until the product sells or you split the revenue.

You can get the rights to products for no money up front by saying you'll try to sell what they have — and if you sell anything, you'll get a percentage.

Do you want to find out more about all of this? Visit my website at **www.nowheretomillionaire.com**.

The most important thing to remember?
Make sure everything you do is 100 percent legal, ethical, and in writing.

CHAPTER 13: How to Tingle the World

So now you have an idea, product, or service you want to bring to market and don't know what to do. I have a product that gives you the information you will need.

Even if you don't want to bring your own product or service to market, read the steps because there will be at least one idea you'll find useful in your current business.

This information is very basic, though, and will not teach you everything. If you want a step-by-step, detailed blueprint of what to do and how to create your whole system, visit my site, **www.nowheretomillionaire.com**. Click on the "Products" link and read about the *Show Me The Money Success System*.

I have a phenomenal team available to coach you — because I want nothing more than to see you succeed. They will take you through the process, step-by-step, so you understand how to start with an idea and grow it to make money.

Schedule a free consultation to review where you are and where you want to be. Just go to my site and sign up while it is on your mind!

I'm going to give you a list of considerations or questions you can ask yourself once you've come up with an idea that seems fresh. Know that this will cost you money and is a business with a lot of complicated steps.

If you have an idea now, think of it as you go through this list. If it feels like you can handle these steps or outsource them to others — and you have some money or know how to raise it — then I encourage you to go for it.

This stream of income is not for the faint of heart or for people who are easily rejected, don't like to follow up, or are broke. It can be very lucrative.

You don't need to be the smartest tack in the bunch to succeed —
nor do you have to have the best or most complicated idea.

Think of the Pet Rock, the Slinky©, the Hula Hoop, dental floss, Post-Its®, or The Tingler™. These are all multimillion-dollar ideas that you could have thought of, right?

I'm sure there have been times when you've said, "I've got a great idea that I know will sell." Then you do nothing. Meanwhile, someone else makes the millions — you buy it knowing you originally thought of that idea.

If you have a great idea, the time to act is now!

NOTE: I am not a lawyer. Speak to one before implementing these ideas or systems. This is what we did. It may work for you, it may not. Invent your own system and use this outline in any way that serves you best.

IDEA FOR PRODUCT

It's in your dreams, haunting you. You have an idea that must be implemented — and you feel you are the one to do it. Your single desire is on fire. People around you say you're nuts, but it's a genius idea that they would buy. They even hand you the cash in desperation for your invention.

You feel like you are the reincarnated Tesla or Edison — you're sure you've got a winner and you've chosen to take action. Here are some questions to answer so you can make sure you've done the background research.

There are invention groups on- and off-line designed to help everyone from the newbie to the experienced inventor. You can join them to get more insights on these questions. This is important because you'll need specialized knowledge to fulfill your organized plan and take immediate action.

They will help you decide if your idea is unique and inexpensive enough to make a profit after you've manufactured it.

If you need help manufacturing, securing intellectual rights, or any other part of bringing your idea, service, or product to market, you can contact me through my website and get the help you need. If I can't do it myself, I have someone I can recommend to help you.

This is where your invention groups also come in handy. You post your question to the group, and often within minutes someone will recommend an individual or a company that is ready and able to move you forward.

> **WARNING: There are a lot of scammers out there! Be careful. Check recent references and current successes! Don't pay all up front and check guarantees, milestones, measurable results, etc.**

This list you are about to receive took hundreds of thousands of dollars and a huge learning curve to develop. You are getting it for the small investment you made to purchase the book. I have sold it by itself for $197. This is my gift to you for taking on your life *big time*!

Allow me a moment of transparency here. I trust that you are starting to understand that I overdeliver, give huge value, and want us to work together all our lives. Know that in the future, I will have other products, coaching and live events. I will be promoting other high-quality, top-value products and services. Who knows, maybe one day it will be your service or product, right?

So I'm asking you now, please, open my e-mails to you, take advantage of live events and webinars — some will be free, some will cost a little, and some will make you gasp. All of it will be worth it. Promise you will keep learning, growing, supporting others, and helping dreams come true. If we all work together, we will succeed easier and more brilliantly than if we try it alone.

And please share my message with everyone you know, too. I honestly want to create a powerful movement — that's the best way I know to do it!

MILLION–DOLLAR REINVENTION QUESTIONS

1. Has your idea ever been done, and if so, can you improve upon it? You need to change the invention by at least 10 to 20 percent to call it a new invention. Could it be smaller, lighter, packed with more features, made digital, given a new design, or distributed differently?

2. Is there a market for it? Who? How big? Search online to find out how many people look for the niche in which you want to design/invent. There needs to be at least a few thousand people searching monthly for the product or something similar. Personally, I like a niche that has at least 100,000 searching for it monthly.

3. What problem does it solve? You are going for a mass market, ideally, because it is often expensive and time-consuming to develop and market a new product.

4. Is there anything like it on market? Who is the "competition" and how successful are they? Are they a well-known brand? Could you sell the idea to them?

5. What is unique about your product? If it is not unique, it might not sell as well because competition will lower your profit margin. Check online to get the best price and the most market share — be sure you compete on price versus quality and value. Consider that most people are looking for the best deal regardless of quality.

6. Where will it be sold? Know ahead of time if your product or service will be marketable worldwide or locally. If you will market locally, you may want to find out about your potential clients/ customers and ask questions so you are clear on issues local individuals are regularly trying to solve and what they want to pay for the solution. Take pre-orders from local stores, giving confidence to investors and vendors.

    WARNING: The more you tell and show, the more it's possible that someone could take your idea. Always have them sign a non-disclosure and/or a non-compete form. If they end up manufacturing and don't pay you royalties, you have written proof you showed them the idea first.

7. Has your idea been patented? Check at **www.uspto.gov**. Even if it has, you can speak with the patent owner and get paid to market it. You will have a lot of ideas from this book they won't know about.

8. Create, design, and name your product. Test it — do people like the name? Get a website with the name — ideally a dot com since more people still search for a .com than any other domain choice (.net, .biz., .mobi, .me, .info, .org, etc.).

9. Trademark the name of the product or service. Think of the value of names like Google, Microsoft, Pepsi or McDonalds. A trademark ensures that, for a limited time, no one else can use the name. Check online for websites already using the name — if you find none, take it as a good first sign. Visit **www.uspto.gov** and search trademarks to see if it has been registered. Be aware that the site can be a bit behind — even if you don't find anything, someone else may have recently applied for a trademark that has yet to post. There may also be a variety of applicable categories.

10. Copyright if you can. This will cost less than $50 and will protect you better, faster, and cheaper than getting a patent. It's also much easier to defend in court.

11. If your idea doesn't qualify for a copyright, get patent-pending status by getting a provisional patent. A patent is a 20-year monopoly hold on a product. You can license your product and make a royalty. You can check online to find out more, but basically you pay a few hundred dollars to hold a position in line for a design or utility patent. This lets you test your design, find a market for it, and possibly get investors. It often takes a few years to get a patent; they are very, very expensive to defend, and you have to defend it to keep it. Get insurance — if it's available — because people and companies will knock you off if your product becomes a success. This represents the underbelly of the invention business.

12. Hire a top intellectual-property attorney — and don't skimp! Make sure they are a trial attorney, too, since you may need to defend your patent. See if you can find someone who has worked as a reviewer within the patent office because they have the extra, winning insights you will need.

13. Have your invention made into a prototype. Who will design and create it? Use the Internet to source options and check with your new inventor friends, forums, groups, meet-ups, etc. You want to find an ethical company who believes in your product so much that they pay to create the prototype then expect to be paid back and make money on their investment. They may amortize the cost of the prototype and ask you to buy a minimum so they not only get paid back but also make a profit for taking the risk. Big manufacturers often have deals with the large chain stores and international sources.

14. How much will it cost per unit? How much for design, mold, and product? Be sure to pad your estimate a bit because things always cost more than what was quoted — you want to be prepared. You can always overestimate and ensure that you are making money at the higher rate so you are protected. It will be great news when it turns out more profitable than you planned. Everything goes up yearly — sometimes more often. Our product was copper, and the price of raw goods more than doubled in months, not years.

15. Is it profitable? Five to one is ideal ($4 is your cost, $20 is the retail price); four to one is okay. Don't break this rule — it's just not worth it. Retailers will double your price; and kiosks, infomercials, MLM companies, and other venues will want to buy cheaply.

16. Find a manufacturer. If you live in the U.S. and have an American manufacturer, be aware that it is often more expensive than using one that's overseas — but there are advantages. You won't wait as long to get your shipment — it can take a month or more to ship from China. You can often buy less to start. You give jobs to local people. It is more complicated to import or export goods, and there are often taxes — it can be a hassle to get a product from overseas to where you or your warehouse might be. Your product will go through customs, which means it may get stopped, held up, or sent back to the factory. There are quality-control matters, human right issues, and environmental concerns, too. You will be expected to pay for at least half up front.

Also know that you will likely be responsible for getting a mold made. This can be expensive and can take a long time to go from conception to completion. Shipping samples are costly, and there is always the chance that the prototype will not work or be cost-effective. Always get the cost of the mold and individual units in writing. Make sure you will not be charged more for any reason, and that you will only pay if the order comes in on time.

17. Design the packaging. You'll need to hire a graphic artist and a copywriter — locally or overseas — and you'll need photos. Be sure to get references and prices ahead of time, as well as samples of their work. Be certain that the work is theirs and not that of an old partner or colleague. Visit my site at **www.nowheretomillionaire.com** to find bidders for the job.

18. Get orders. Pre-sell your product then create it after you have enough people ready to pay for it now — at a price for which you know you will make a profit. Get letters of intent and testimonials from these individuals — this will impress buyers, vendors, and/ or investors by creating a strong demand.

19. Know the turnaround time. How long will it take to test the prototype, tweak it, and get it shipped and into stores or your distribution centers? Unless your name is Rip Van Winkle, you want your product *ASAP*.

20. Set up a merchant account — you want to be able to accept credit cards. Getting a merchant account can be difficult, depending on your credit and experience; sometimes banks won't give you one until you have a track record. Use **www.paypal.com**. It's easy to create an account and start taking money fast.

21. Get permits, a resell license, DBA, etc. Check your local laws and the Small Business Association. You'll find them all online — they have the answers to what is needed to be *too legit to quit*.

22. Create a legal entity. Check with an attorney and accountant to see what is right for you. You may want to create an LLC, a C-Corp, or an S-Corp, depending on your business model. They all have advantages and disadvantages — you need to know the tax laws to see which will work best for you, save you the most money, have the best asset protection, and leave you least liable for anything...except looking gorgeous as you, of course.

23. Once you get manufacturing, check into product liability insurance and get at least $1,000,000 worth. Also look into patent-protection insurance or Intellectual Property protection insurance, and officers insurance, in case someone sues you. They will be much less likely to go after you if they know you are

insured. Be aware that most insurance companies will drop you after a suit (or threat of a suit).

24. Create nondisclosure, noncompete sales and distribution forms. You'll find templates and samples of a lot of the necessary forms online. You can check with sales or distribution companies to see what forms they use. Ask an attorney to make sure they will work for you in your state. You will need to do some extra homework if you plan to work overseas.

    A non-disclosure form is designed to protect you when you show your designs or prototypes to others. The sales forms will give the buyer your terms and conditions, including product price and minimum order size. It will have pictures of the products, often with testimonials or endorsements from people who like the product, and other pertinent information like shipping options and your contact information.

25. Hire a graphic artist (or rehire the one who designed your packaging). You need to create a company identity — logos, stationery, business cards, etc. Find someone who can visually reflect who you are and what your product or service is. You want to make a good first impression so people want what you have.

26. Get a website and hire a web designer if you are unable to design the site yourself. Be sure to display the product well, with photos of people actually using it. You'll need video, audio, and sales copy — again, outsource if you're not strong at this. Set it up so you can take orders online and make it easy to do so — test it, then have others test it and buy a product. Think of the whole cycle — seeing it, buying it, shipping it, following up with the buyer, and selling them more. Give value, create rapport, and be generous — this will result in buyers who refer others to you. Make sure to use Web 2.0 or 3.0 tools as well as blogs, articles, PR, Facebook, Twitter, LinkedIn, MySpace, and any other social networking tools you can think of.

27. Create buzz! It can take three to six months or more to get magazines to print a blurb or an article about your product. The easiest way to speed up the process is to find celebrities to endorse your product or take a photo using it. Once you've selected a celebrity, send your product to their press person,

asking them to get it in front of their famous client. You can also give one to a writer, a bodyguard, a makeup artist, the person responsible for props or costumes...whatever it takes, do it.

Sometimes press will not sell the products for you — and that can be disappointing. Try to remember that *any* press is better than none, then seek out new avenues to get the buzz going. Go online and search for press services like **www.prnewswire.com**. Fee-based services will get your word out to a much larger audience, but you'll also find many free service providers. Submit a press release. Get good placement in the search engines by using popular *keywords* people input into online searches. Keyword-dense releases have a better shot at being on page one, which in turn guarantees more traffic to your site. If it has great copy, pictures, video, audio, testimonials, and an attractive price, you *will* sell the product from the press you get.

28. Test online. It's faster and cheaper to see which headline, copy, or photo brings the best results. Test and get your conversion rates. How many people see the ad before they buy it? One to three percent is a typical low-end figure. Do the math — how many products do you need to sell to make it profitable?

29. How much will it cost you to get the customer? What are they worth long-term? This will help you decide how much you can afford to spend on marketing and give you a better idea of which techniques might work for you. Offline, online, voice broadcasts, fax broadcasts, teleclasses, webinars, trade shows, ads, banners — once you find the sweet spot, you will have a built-in ATM machine automatically depositing large checks into your bank!

30. Find sales representatives and distributors. Do this online or attend trade shows and look at showrooms. Ask the management to introduce you to reps. Always speak with their other clients to make sure they are aggressive. Do they have the kind of accounts you need to succeed? Do they have enough reps? Are they good at what they do? Many will tell a great story to get you to sign, then do nothing for you. Often they will recruit you before a big, expensive trade show — which means you pay a lot for a booth plus 15 percent of all sales that are written during the show. You will have to fly out,

work the booth, sell your product, take the order, give it to them — then they make money on that sale and all sales after that as long as they are your rep. Make sure they have a well-visited showroom, serve food and drinks during the show, give away prizes, and have a large invite list of big buyers to make it worth your while. This is when you meet most of the people who will buy from you.

31. Get a toll-free number so people can easily call to obtain information about your company or product, place orders, or inquire about returns or exchanges. You need to take care of the whole process if you don't have a sales rep or distributor. You can certainly outsource this task, but be sure you choose wisely since they are the first voice your customer will hear. Role play and pretend to buy your product so you can experience their sales practice firsthand. You want to be sure your customers are well respected, their sales are closed, and that they consistently buy more than they originally planned.

32. Get an account with UPS or FedEx. If you are going to be doing your own shipping, try to get cheaper shipping rates or find a good fulfillment company and call center to take orders for you. Bicoastal? Focus your efforts on companies in the middle of the country for faster shipping.

These are some of the basics to consider. Now can you see why I have a whole program on what to do? I include systems for optimal efficiency — that's where this checklist originated. It is a very small part of a whole system based on making costly mistakes so you can avoid them.

I also discuss how to hire an attorney, accountant, and the rest of your team. What else will you learn?

- How to save money on taxes
- How to create a legal entity
- What is a patent, a trademark, and a copyright; and who to hire to set them up for you
- How to get money for your ideas — and have investors *begging* to do business with you

If those things interest you, make sure to check out my "Show Me The Money" invention package. It will answer most — if not all — of your questions and take you by the hand from conception to completion of your product, service, or idea. Oh, yeah...and you'll learn how to make money, too.

To get a Tingler head massager — for you and as a great gift —
go to www.nowheretomillionaire.com and pick one up today.

Imagine being able to say the same thing in a book; on your site; or on the radio, online, on Facebook, Twitter, Myspace, TV, at a family reunion, on a shopping network, in a catalog, in the newspaper, on a popular blog, in a press release, to a joint venture partner, to an affiliate, or to a distributor.

How about in an article on an article directory (for example, go to **www.articlecity.com**)? This lets you translate your article into 30 languages, re-tweet it, connect to Facebook, and use RSS feeds and the top social networks to syndicate your article so it immediately gets read internationally.

There are so many ways to get your product, idea, or service directly to the people who already want what you have!

EASIEST WAY TO GET A PRODUCT TO MARKET

1. Find a unique product with a patent but no successful sales record — or take your own ready-to-manufacture or already-being-manufactured product. Tie up the rights, become a distributor, or negotiate a joint venture deal with the inventor.

2. Create a video of it and your story and upload your pitch to me at **www.nowheretomillionaire.com**.

3. If it's a viable idea, I may get it to my team to market it with you.

PRACTICE

1. Follow the checklist and invent a product.
2. Call my coaching team and get a free consultation today.

You can get the "Show Me The Money Success System" at my website (**www.nowheretomillionaire.com**). Click on "Products" for information that will tell you whether it's right for you. You can order 24/7, download it to have access immediately, or get the physical product — a 300-page notebook with more than six hours of critical information. You don't need the checklist — I gave it to you in this book!

I am in the process, as I write this, of creating a system that shows you exactly what to do if your product is complete and you want to market it on- and offline.

CHAPTER 14: You, Sex, Power, and Millionaires

I think I got hired as an expert, coach, and mentor on the TV series with my friend Kelly Ripa because I get fast, dramatic results. I show women inventors how to pitch their product to Home Shopping Network (HSN) — what a huge opportunity for a lucky few! I offer tough love, strategies, tactics, a hug, and laughter, just like I do in this book.

To prepare for the experience, I read thousands of books, blogs, and articles; I've practiced pitching and giving talks; and I've failed and succeeded often enough to understand what seems to work and what doesn't. I am humbled and honored to see so many testimonials from clients and students who have learned and succeeded by working together. I look forward to hearing from you!

SOME INSPIRATION

Named one of America's "Power Women" by *Ladies Home Journal*, Stacey Schieffelin, a former Ford model, is a down-to-earth, authentic, vibrant, highly successful entrepreneur. She is the founder and President of ybf (your best friend) and has created a 14-year record of success in direct sales on Home Shopping Network (HSN). She started with no money and a dream — yet now has a huge, loyal, and worldwide consumer base of women with cosmetic and apparel sales in excess of $150 million!

I was fortunate enough to work with Stacey on the series *Homemade Millionaire*. We became instant friends. I asked her to give you some secret insights into how to possibly get your product on HSN and, once you do, how to sell your dream so it's wildly successful! Since her mission is to empower women, she said, "Yes!!!"

I'm proud to be part of the HSN family; I'm humbled and honored to know that it reaches potentially 90 million viewers! Your goal is to get on HSN, right? I feel you. So please accept these words of wisdom — Stacey's four decrees for success — as you dream, set your goals and prepare to make your million(s) by being in genuine service to others, remaining an individual with integrity, offering huge value, always under-promising and over-delivering like Stacey does.

FOUR DECREES FOR SUCCESS

Great Product: Don't create ME TOO's — be original! Do your research. Find out which products have been the most successful on air in your category. Think about a non-obvious way to extend the brand messaging to where you have a strong point of distinction.

Great Story: Why did you create your dream product? Was it something that you couldn't find anywhere else? Was there something in your childhood or family history that brought you to this place? Was the product the result of years of research performed in your kitchen or garage? Was it in response to a major organization that just wouldn't listen?

Great Demonstration: What is the three-sentence message your audience will remember when the credit-card bill comes and they think, "Now why did I need this?" Make sure you can articulate the message simply on air. You only have a few minutes, so the demonstration needs to be a show-stopper. Think of what you can do that really shows off your product — and do it in 20 seconds.

Great Storyteller: The fact that you are a great inventor does not necessarily mean you are the one who can best represent your story on TV. You have four minutes to become a product star, so make sure the person on air can speak from the heart but also understands the importance of delivering a strong message and presentation. If you love it, you can sell it.

I'm sure you are thinking, "Stacey probably had connections or money." Well, think again. She had no money when she started. Thanks to a receptive and flexible American Express representative who happened to be a lover of fine cosmetics, she was able to creatively finance her first purchase of products for a kit she sold on HSN in 1996. It all started with one unexpected "Yes" and has evolved into an incredible business — with over 1,000 different products sold in more than five countries. The truth is, if she can do it, you can, too!

If excuses are starting to pop into your head, remember that you have the choice to either make excuses or have the life of your dreams! Which would you prefer?

HOW TO PITCH:
A ROAD MAP TO THE AMERICAN DREAM

You've got a million-dollar idea. It's simple. It doesn't cost much to make it. There is a real need for it. You have a new twist on an old idea. You can make life easier, less expensive, more fun, sexier, more powerful, or more efficient. There is a captive market and future vision. You sure have a winner, right?

Now imagine that you have four to five minutes to pitch your idea at a rate of $5,000 a minute. How will you pitch your product or idea knowing it will cost you anywhere from $20 to $25,000?

Remember, the brain is lazy — keep things easy and
simple to understand. Think Homer Simpson.

The simplest way to keep it easy to remember is to make your pitch and demonstration very visual — make it experiential. Paint pictures. For instance, if your product is fire retardant, light it on fire. If your product is unbreakable, throw it at a wall across the room. Show dramatic before-and-after pictures, because people love to see immediate or startling results. The more theatrical you make it, the more memorable it will be! Have a *wow* factor!

Believe in yourself and your story.

What does the product's solution represent for your buyer? Be sure to do your homework. What do these buyers buy, and why? What are their needs, and do you fit them? You must be able to succinctly show how your products meet the needs of the buyer. Find out by asking them, and have your own answers.

They want to know how they will make money with your product, that if they invest in you, you'll have great follow-through, be true to your word, be easy to work with, keep inventing, add to your line, etc. Think collections — expand your line to build your estrogen empire. You are building a brand, meaning a great expansive story so people relate and think of you first.

Be outrageous and memorable!!! Zany, funny, crazy!

Let's run through a series of questions and considerations to help you devise your pitch.

INITIAL CONSIDERATIONS

1. Does your product provide a better way to _____?

2. What does your product do?

3. What problems does it solve? (The potential buyer doesn't care about the product; they care about the problem it solves!)

4. How is it different from other products on the market?

5. Why should the buyer care?

6. What does the buyer value? This is the most important one. Find out their pain; solve it in a way that gets them to act now.

CREATE A GOOD PITCH

1. Be well rehearsed, informative, entertaining, and inspirational.

2. Remember to be authentic, genuine, natural, conversational.

3. Have a great story. Tell your audience who you are, how you created the product, what problem you were trying to solve, and how great your life is now that you have your solution.

4. Relate to your audience — engage them!

5. Present an appealing, passionate, must-have-this experience.

6. Sell the dream of a better life — after all, aren't you really selling the dream of a better future? Sell dreams, not products. Will they be healthier, make more money, save time? Sell the experience.

7. Have a profound sense of mission.

8. Make people fall in love with your vision.

9. Have passion, persuasion, energy, and charisma. Love your product!

10. Demonstrate how your product improves lives.

11. Entertain and delight so people want what you offer.

12. Spark the imagination of those listening.

13. Demonstrate how you can extend or expand your line, your brand. Is it a collection? An empire? The first product of many?

14. Spend time considering the rational explanation for why buyers are emotionally driven to things.

BE PERSUASIVE!

1. Deliver a story that gets immediate interest — test and rehearse, ask for feedback, use focus groups of potential buyers.

2. Pose a problem or question that needs to be solved or answered.

3. Offer a unique solution to the problem.

4. Give specific benefits for your product. "What this means for you is..."

5. State a call to action — "Buy one now," "Invest now," "Limited time or limited offer," or "Free shipping if you order now." Ask your buyer to do something now!

THE POWER OF THREE

As you are preparing to write your pitch, draw an easy-to-follow map.

People can remember three points. I learned that back in my high school speech and debate classes; it seems to be widely accepted. Let's be honest here, most of us can't even remember what we had for dinner last night. We are inundated with too much input and after a few ideas, we are overwhelmed or simply shut down.

Keep that in mind when you're considering your audience. It's likely they'll be multitasking while attempting to hear you — they text, instant message, check e-mails, and are kind of hearing you. So you need to figure out the three points that are the most riveting, spellbinding, fascinating, enthralling, entrancing, mesmerizing, exhilarating, and thrilling!!!

Here is what you can say when you are making the points:

My first story is _____ and what it means to you is _____. My second story is _____ and what it means to you is _____. My third story is _____ and what it means to you is _____.

Tell a *wow* story and create a stunning conclusion that leads to gotta-have-it-now results. Focus on the key points and use repetition so people remember exactly what you want them to remember.

1.   List all the key points you want the buyers to know about your product.

2.   Get the list down to three ideas — this will be the majority of your pitch.

3.   Each idea needs to tell a story and use analogies, metaphors, facts, and/or testimonials.

4.   Tell your audience the three things you want them to take away.

5.   Give them a directive and tell them to take action.

AN EXCITING STORY

Your story has to have compelling messages, be clear, and remain fun. Here are some ways to help you do just that.

1.   Create a catchy headline.

Think Twitter, where you get 140 characters or a short one-liner. Keep it ten words or less and make it memorable. Here are some examples: A vacation in a bottle. Business in a box. Tingle the world. Happiest place on Earth.

2.   Know your market.

What is your niche? What are the demographics? Is it a million-dollar market? Research your market and know it well.

3.   Be aware of the "big picture."

How big is the industry? Online travel is a $90 billion industry. Pets is a $30 billion industry in just the U.S. "Life is good" T-shirts and other products are worth $80 million. How big is the diet industry? How big is the market you are interested in? Again, research it and know it well.

4.   Have an understanding of the customer's "pain."

What does the customer need? Talk about the problem that once made you say, "There has to be a better way and I'm going to invent it." Tell the personal story. Paint a picture.

Focus on the pain and relate it to the buyer. The worse it is and the more they can identify with it as the adversary, the better you set yourself up to solve the problem.

5. Present a solution.

    Cure the pain. You are the hero — you make lives better. Prove that you save the consumer from the opponent. You make things right. Tell a personal story about the solution.

You have three main points to get your story across — no more than that. Answer the problems you just brought up.

What is your edge? How are you a vision for the future? What is the dream and how does your product create fast results?

Who specifically will buy your product? Mention them in your stories. If it's a diverse cross-section of people, use them in your story to expand your niche.

SEVEN THINGS TO BE SURE YOU HAVE

1. Experience with the product or industry
2. A product with a great, memorable name (branding)
3. Awesome packaging
4. A superb price point, huge profit margin (5 to 10 times for a physical product, 100+ times for an informational product)
5. An experienced team, and mentors
6. A domain name for your product and a website
7. A provisional patent, trademark, copyrights

EVERYONE LOVES A GREAT SHOW!

1. Show how easy the product is to use, how functional it is, how much value there is, how many others love it or bought it.
2. Remember that this is the first product of a collection, an empire, a line — your brand.
3. Use descriptive words. Say "Isn't it beautiful?" "Isn't it amazing?" "You can take it with you everywhere, isn't that great?"
4. Practice your demo over and over again. Focus on sounding natural.
5. Make your product stand out. Make it remarkable.

ADDRESSING OBJECTIONS

1. Make a list of all the objections, and have an amazing answer for them.

2. Tell a story of someone objecting to something and how it was handled — turn it into a benefit. Include the objections in your pitch so, ideally, the buyer has no questions. An audience remembers when there's a story behind a product. Additionally, showing the product is more memorable than just talking about it.

URGENCY AND ACTION

1. Create urgency by setting up a limited offer. People buy now if they think they are afraid they might miss or lose something important.

2. Include the headline again. Make your main point the one they walk away with. Then ask them to buy or invest now.

MORE FOR CONSIDERATION

1. How can you make your pitch theatrical to create buzz and genuine awe?

2. What is your story? What's the most important thing for them to walk away with? Repeat that point until the listener gets it.

3. What do you value — what is your purpose beyond making money?

4. How can you paint a passionate picture to which the buyers can relate?

5. What are the main reasons the buyer will love your product?

6. Speak in simple and descriptive English or whatever language you are fluent in. Eliminate the jargon and big words.

7. How can you engage them where they live? Find the human connection! Find the common bond and create immediate rapport.

8. Make sure you are centered and focused before you begin. Create eye contact and smile as long as it's natural.

BREAKING THE PITCH APART

Okay, let's get down to the basics. If you only had 30 seconds, how would you sell me your product? Record yourself making your pitch and play it back. Find three main points to expand upon that are dramatic and tell a great story.

Do you know how to do any magic tricks or celebrity impersonations? Can you juggle, dance, sing, tell jokes? Is there anything that makes you stand out? How about a dramatic demo — can you light something on fire or hit it with a hammer? Do you have before-and-after pictures or videos?

SHOW INTEREST IN THE BUYERS/INVESTORS

1. Introduce yourself.

2. Be genuine.

3. Acknowledge them.

4. Compliment them, if it is sincere.

5. Use their names if you remember them.

ASK QUESTIONS

1. Get them to agree with you at least three times in the first minute of your pitch.

2. Ask questions. *Have you ever wanted to save time as you're getting ready for work? Would you like to stop a headache naturally in ten seconds or less? Can you imagine a life without smelly garbage cans?*

3. Get their buy-in and create rapport. The more someone says "Yes!" in the first minute, the more likely they are to say "Yes!" later.

KEEP THE BIG PICTURE IN MIND

1. How big is the industry?

2. Is this product trendy?

3. Any celebs love your product?

4. How many people search the term online? When you pull up the keyword on Google — how many pages come up?

5. Why is this so popular?

PRESENT THE PROBLEM

What is their pain? Tell them about it. Acknowledging this gets people to listen to you and your solution.

How did this problem affect you? Were there any products to solve the problem? If so, why did you still invent a product? Did you talk to other buyers? What did they say? How much would they pay for it?

1. What is the challenge your buyers face? Ask them. Observe the problem and explain why you have the better way to solve it.

2. Who is your buyer? Who is your market? How big is it?

3. What need is not being met? How can you meet it?

4. Why should they care? It's never about you, it's always about them. Tell them how it saves them time and money; gets their house cleaner; makes them look better, thinner, stronger, or faster.

5. Why do they need this now?

6. Build the pain, make it tangible, make it real — create a vivid picture

7. Create a villain so you can be the hero. Make the buyer rally around you so they will be excited about your instant, affordable solution.

8. Tell a story about a client's "pain" — something the audience can relate to or feel.

9. Tell your own personal story related to the problem — is that why you invented this?

PRESENT THE SOLUTION

Create rapport with buyers — make an emotional connection fast.

1. How does your product add value to buyers' lives?

2. How does your product unleash human potential?

3. Paint a picture of the present and the future, both with and without your product.

4. Burn, stir, propel the vision — you are the one they've been waiting for! You are the savior of the moment.

5. Present the headline, the problem, the solution, the benefits, details, demo, call to action, then repeat the headline.

6. Why do you need this now?

7. Don't sell solutions — create stories!

8. Grab attention! Make it a must-have experience.

9. What do people want? Ask them. Turn their answers into stories.

10. Compare your product to other successful ones. Know how well they did and why yours is better.

A STEP-BY-STEP SOLUTION

1. Start with a headline.

2. Decide what you are inventing or reinventing.

    A. What one line describes it best? Your headline needs to be concise and specific. It needs to offer personal benefit.

    B. Describe your product in ten words or less — you have ten seconds to interest someone. *I tingle the world. There's the Horse and Dog Whisperer; I'm the Authenticity Whi$perer.*

    C. Fill in the blank: "This is a better way to _____." This will help you find your headline fast.

3. Develop a passion statement.

    A. What problem does it solve? "I'm excited about this product because it _____."

    B. What three messages do you want the buyers to remember?

    C. Think in analogies or metaphors, easy comparisons. What is your product like? Answer that question, then repeat so the buyer remembers.

4. Demo, demo, demo!

    A. They might forget what you say, but they won't forget how you make them feel.

    B. You need a big "aha" moment, a memorable moment that is unexpected. Build the moment of surprise — be sure you practice so it's smooth.

CREATE A REVOLUTION

Do you know what Steve Jobs says about Macintosh computers? "Every once in a while a revolutionary product comes along that changes everything." I'm a longtime Mac owner because of that statement.

How are you creating a revolution?

1. A dynamic and fun demo is key. Keep things moving.

2. Create a display with graphics, your logo, pictures of your product — especially ones of other individuals enjoying it. Make sure the display is easy to bring out and really bring it to life. Let them feel it and taste it — make it funny if you can, but be sure it is dramatic.

3. Do something to wow them — add drama! You want them to say, "What a great idea! I wish I would have thought of that!"

4. Have testimonials, word of mouth, success stories, whatever. Who loves your invention? Tell us about it, really paint a picture. Video works well, both on your site and in your pitch.

5. Do you have any helpful props? Use them.

6. Have fun!!!! Be creative! Brains don't pay attention to boring things.

7. Keep it short and simple.

8. What's sensational about your product?

9. Get them to want more. Is it functional? Well priced? Easy to use?

10. Imagine a buyer shouting, "So what?!" Answer it clearly and keep it in mind when you are demonstrating.

11. How does the product work? There is a problem you've identified — how does your product solve it?

12. Use props. Give the buyer something to do, something to experience.

13. Focus on the most memorable benefit.

14. Commit to your demo and be flexible if it doesn't go perfectly. I've seen people lose it because something doesn't work properly. If you are fully prepared and rehearsed, shake off any mishaps and know that you have the ability to stay on track. Make a joke, move on.

15. Make the product look great and easy to use.

BODY LANGUAGE

1. Make eye contact; commit to open postures and gestures, be easygoing and confident, and most important...be yourself.

2. Pacing, pauses, volume, and inflection are basic speaking skills.

3. Create suspense and excitement.

4. Don't rush. Let it breathe.

5. Use fun words — *awesome, unbelievable, the bomb diggity...*

6. Confidence is key!

PRACTICE, PRACTICE, PRACTICE!

1. Use video. Record yourself.

2. Get feedback.

3. Watch for useless words — um, like, ah...

4. Is your body open or defensive, confident, fidgety, distracting? Stiff?

5. Vocal delivery — monotone? Well paced? Excited?

6. Energy — are you vibrant? Enthusiastic? Thrilled, uplifting, inspiring and smiling?

LOOKS *DO* MATTER!

Make sure you look your very best — when we look in the mirror and are happy with what we see, we come off as more confident and secure to others. Get someone to do your hair and makeup.

If you are being televised, wear solid colors since most patterns will appear solid on-camera anyway. Find colors and cuts that bring out your best features.

INVESTOR AND BUYER RESPONSE

At the end of your pitch, investors and buyers will most likely ask you questions. You'll want to keep a few things in mind.

1. Engage in conversation and feel free to ask your own questions.

2. Never apologize.

3. Be respectful.

4. Don't be defensive.

5. Let them know you are easy to work with — a team player.

6. Know everything about the product — any competition, the market and how big it is, whether you're aiming to be trendy, if you have any celebs endorsing.

7. Be honest!

8. Practice your answers so they come out naturally.

9. Do you have an entertaining short story or any good anecdotes to which the buyer can relate? Keep them in mind so you can use them at the appropriate time.

SOME QUESTIONS TO EXPECT

1. Who are you?

2. What is your passion statement?

3. What is your business background? (Or, what is your experience?)

4. What is your idea and why is it unique?

5. What is the cost of the product? Have you obtained cost estimates from several manufacturers?

6. Is it already being manufactured?

7. Where are you in the process?

8. What does the product mean to the buyer?

9. What problems does it solve?

10. Is it a new idea or an enhancement to another product?

11. Have you researched the price, packaging, and selling methods of similar products?

12. Who is your competition? How much market share do they have?

13. How are you different from them?

14. Why would you be great for a shopping channel? (Or, why do you want to be on the shopping channel?)

15. Where do you want to be five or ten years from now?

16. How do we know you'll stick with this goal?

17. How are sales doing in your product category?

18. Who are your potential customers? What is their average age? What other products do they buy? What do they care about?

19. Are you prepared to succeed?

20. Have you created a business budget?

21. Do you have any funding?

22. How much money or help do you need?

23. Do you have a business and marketing plan?

24. Do you have mentors?

25. Are you involved in local business networking opportunities?

26. Do you go to seminars or workshops to meet other inventors or buyers of your product?

27. Do you use social media — Facebook, Twitter, LinkedIn, Meetup? Do you have a blog or a website? Do you write articles?

28. Have you created a legal entity to protect your assets?

29. Do you have a provisional patent, trademark, or copyright?

30. Do you have a lawyer, accountant, and dream team?

31. Is your domain name the same as your product?

32. Do you have a logo?

33. Is your packaging design complete?

34. What is missing from your prototype?

35. Have you tested your product in different markets?

36. Have you done any sales?

37. What do local retailers think of your product?

38. Do you have a media kit?

39. Have you sent out stories about your product?

40. Have you ever done a trade show?

CHAPTER 15:
Zsa Zsa's Laws of Attraction and Money

"I'm an excellent housekeeper. Every time I get a divorce, I keep the house."
— Zsa Zsa Gabor

I think she was married something like 327 times...so, yeah, she did pretty well. You will do well, too, once you understand the secrets behind the secret. Think of yourself as a broadcaster and receiver of the Abundant Seven Spiritual Truths.

THE ABUNDANT SEVEN SPIRITUAL TRUTHS

SOURCE/SPIRIT IS YOU.
THAT WHICH CREATES ALL CREATES YOU.

You are not a mistake. You are perfect and whole. You create everything in your life. Your good depends on you — not on outside people, circumstances, places, or things.

You think you have little influence on outside events — that thought is an illusion. You are the individualized expression of the infinite. You get to give God/Source a good time as it is animated through you, as you.

If you have *faith* in the energy that creates everything — including the air you breathe — and allow yourself to become steeped in that energy, that soup, that breath, then you will understand that you are truly limitless.

Imagine that for a moment.

If you really believe that, only your old conversations or past can de-motivate you into a warped small reality.

ABUNDANCE IS A HERE-AND-NOW REALITY

Can you count all the stars? Every grain of sand? Each blade of grass? Your every breath? Nope. They are limitless and endless — and there are limitless, endless variations and possibilities.

Your life can be an endless moment-to-moment celebration of the here and now. It can be about celebrating the infinite — or not, it's your choice. If you are choosing to be stuck, you get to remind your mind to look beyond appearances.

Seek to reveal the prosperity that is everywhere — find it, expect it, cherish it, give it, be generous, explore it, love it, desire it, create with it!

ABUNDANCE IS INEXHAUSTIBLE

Creation is an ongoing activity to which you are committed to — and you are doing it constantly. Many times you may be unconscious. Now you choose to be aware.

A flower's seeds germinate, grow, bloom, seed themselves, then die. The process is repeated endlessly. Stars and galaxies do that, too. So do people and circumstances.

Everything visible comes from the invisible. Your life is pure potential and endless possibilities. Everything is fleeting, changing constantly. Your life is a verb, not a noun. All your needs are met because you say so. You declare it.

You rejoice in your potential and are not attached to any of it. You share and remind yourself that you can't out-give. What you give away with an open heart in faith and trust comes back to you. It is the *law of circulation*.

SOURCE MEETS YOUR EVERY NEED AT EVERY MOMENT ACCORDING TO YOUR OWN ACCEPTANCE.

The laws always work, whether you are conscious of them or not. You can ignore or deny or think the laws don't apply to your life, but the truth is that *they do.*

If you desire to be rich in every aspect of your life, it is time to be accepting. You are given the gift of infinite possibilities — you get to decide what you will open up to.

Some come to the river to get a drink and bring a thimble, and some find a way to create endless source through giving and receiving.

What you believe, you can conceive of.

If you want to attract, you want to give a lot. What are you giving, how, to whom? Time, talent, financial resources, energy, attention, love — whatever it is, bring intention and awareness to every aspect of your life.

PRACTICE GIVING YOURSELF FULLY TO LIFE!

Whew, that's a big one. I'll give you a teeny example. Pretend you are in a class and the teacher asks, "By a show of hands, how many of you want to be rich?" Do you raise your hand halfway or stretch it up high? Do you jump up, get on the table, shout wildly, and do a funny dance?

How you do anything is how you do everything. It's time for unreasonable passion!

Oh, and don't look for payoffs from your giving. Live and give with joy, generosity — trust, relax, and let go. Trust that you live in, and create, an abundant universe.

By the way, do you believe in fairies?

EVERYONE DESERVES ABUNDANCE!

Lack and limitation are ideas we seem to reinforce as though they are the truth. They are not — unless we believe it.

If you feel that you deserve abundance, abundance is yours.

Heal your consciousness now. You will be part of the solution, not the problem, by believing this. Your good doesn't detract from others. You don't need to feel guilty or undeserving, because you are choosing to attract the abundance that is natural and plentiful.

You deserve unlimited abundance. Everyone does. Celebrate it and inspire others to seize opportunities to support everyone in becoming wealthy. TO DO THIS, YOU MUST LOVE YOURSELF COMPLETELY AND UNCONDITIONALLY.

You get to forgive yourself, your past, and your stories. Remind yourself you are deserving and worthy of all good things. Extend this awareness to others.

The world you create for yourself and others is based on healing your old interpretations of your worth. Know you are worthy, and teach others to feel the same way. There will be no poverty if we are focused on the solution of self-love and infinite possibilities.

I was sitting in a cute cafe full of homemade food in a charming ski valley close to Taos, New Mexico. It was crazy gorgeous out. A few people asked if they could join me where I was sitting. They asked what I was doing, and I said I was writing this book.

One of the guys said to me, "I'd rather be happy than have money."

I realize that this is a common misconception. People seem to think you can't have both. Let me ask you, how prosperous do you think he is? I reminded him that he's one thought away from getting both. He got it. He bought my tea. Yep! It's an abundant and happy and safe world!

YOUR VISION IS YOUR INNER AWARENESS OF YOUR NATURALLY ABUNDANT SELF

I personally invite you to your greatness. Welcome to your dream. Something in you right now is willing and able to push through any limiting beliefs — and this will lift you into your magnificence. Trust in that vision. It is telling you about the person you are meant to be.

You were not put onto the earth to struggle or to be steeped in adversity, suffering, lack, or misery. You are here to discover who you are in growth, love, and unlimited abundance.

You choose — as the universe does — to expand and to grow. Your vision will unfold based on your being able to see. What you can accept is who you are. There is a new vision that asks you to risk everything to accept your personal greatness. Your false beliefs are simply that: false.

YOUR INNER GUIDANCE WILL LEAD YOU
TOWARD THE FULFILLMENT OF YOUR VISION

Listen to your inner guidance, intuition, synchronicities, and coincidences. Listen to your inner voice, the one that tells you there is a certain "knowing" within you worth paying attention to. Listen. Where are you being directed?

Nothing is insignificant. You may be facing adversity, feeling restriction, or feeling stuck, or are unsure of what to do. There may be resistance — remember, resistance is futile.

Focus on what feeds and nourishes you. You are a co-creator with Spirit — defer to Infinite Intelligence. You will be able to overcome and face your challenges. Consider the uses of adversity.

"Now they show you how detergents take out bloodstains, a pretty violent image there. I think if you've got a T-shirt with a bloodstain all over it, maybe laundry isn't your biggest problem. Maybe you should get rid of the body before you do the wash."
— **Jerry Seinfeld**

SOME MORE UNIVERSAL LAWS

1. **The Law of Cause and Effect.** For every action there is a reaction. If you consistently do the things that you need to succeed, you will succeed. If you don't, you won't.

2. **Nature is neutral.** The stories you tell about events, circumstances, and people are just stories based on your filters, thoughts, beliefs, experiences, and past — they are not real.

3. **You are manufacturing your reality.** You make up your reality moment by moment. You are the author. You must learn to take full responsibility for every aspect of your life.

4. **Nobody is smarter or better than you.** Control your thoughts because comparison just leads to suffering and is not real. These thoughts become excuses for you to stay in your small comfort zone. You sell yourself short and fail to own your greatness — but you can easily learn all the principles, have the thoughts, create new beliefs, find courage, and own your greatness if you choose to.

5. **To succeed you need to have a "no matter what" attitude.** Most people quit too early, after just a few tries. They don't want to feel rejected and doubt if they can do it, so it is easy to give up and say, "I tried." The trick is to be persistent and unstoppable.

6. **Act "As If."** Start with the end in mind and pretend *now* that you've accomplished what you set out to do. It's a big-time success. Now imagine what you did to succeed and work your way back so you know what action to take. From there, you can easily monitor whether that action is working or if you need to tweak the strategies or tactics.

7. **Have a big enough WHY.** How many of you could create an extra $10,000 quickly if someone you loved needed surgery to live? Usually if you choose to give to others — to be in service — you will know why you are doing what you are doing and when you want to quit. You will be aware because you have something big at stake.

8. **Give yourself permission to dream, and act on your dreams.** Taking immediate action and implementing your ideas is crucial. Most people talk and don't act — those who succeed do so because they take action in spite of their fears. You were challenged when you got this book to change your life in three days. What has changed for you?

Your invitation is to watch your thoughts — to notice them — and to pay attention. Who is the thinker behind the thoughts? What do you obsess on? What do your thoughts believe? Are they right? How are they working for you?

Based on results, you will know if you love what you do, live your life purpose, are financially free, spend time doing what you want, give back, live healthy, and focus your thoughts on the positive. If you are all these things, you are in a rich place.

If not, there's no need to judge yourself. Just see the chance to shift, to change, to open up to possibilities — and to fall in love with yourself and the world you are creating.

Remember, we make meaning constantly. Everything is neutral and you give it meaning. Give it meaning that serves you. Watch what happens as you align with positive thoughts.

Be kind to yourself. Celebrate often! You deserve it!

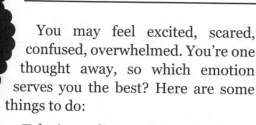

CONCLUSION:
Now What Do You Do?

You may feel excited, scared, confused, overwhelmed. You're one thought away, so which emotion serves you the best? Here are some things to do:

1. Take immediate action toward your dreams.

2. Answer the questions.

3. Do your practices.

4. Create a mastermind on- and offline.

5. Go to my website (**www.nowheretomillionaire.com**) and become a member. Free membership is available — or you can pay for it if you're interested in the VIP stuff.

6. Remember that I have coaching available. I am here to take you by the hand and show you how to implement what you just learned.

7. Continue to grow and learn and support others.

8. Share this so we create a huge international movement.

Experience and embrace radical shifts in every aspect of your now vibrant, authentic life. Now that you have a millionaire mind-set, you can overcome limiting beliefs with practical step-by-step blueprints showing you exactly how to make millions. Make sure to do sensational things for strangers, and serve your clients well!

If you are still pondering, questioning, linked to your past, and contemplating or procrastinating, then good-bye and good luck.

Now that you've experienced yourself more real than ever before, you are ready to tackle finding or deepening your relationships with a soul mate, loving yourself, and making money.

I look forward to connecting, intersecting, uprooting, animating, vividly recalling, breathing, loving, mischievous mysteries unraveling together in our extraordinary travels!

With great respect, honor, and humility,

Wendy Robbins

P.S. — Here is one of my favorite quotes from the Upanishads:

"Radiant is my heart. Spirit lives inside all that is and all that is not, the end of love longing, beyond understanding, the highest in all beings.

Self luminous in me rests all worlds and all beings. My head is fire. My eyes, the sun and moon — my ears — heaven, sacred images and prayers — my words, my breath — the wind, the whole universe, my heart. The earth — my imagination.

I am the spirit in all things. I am beyond time, beyond the world of desire, sorrow is left behind. I embrace joy. My self is smaller then the smallest atom, greater then the largest spaces. I am infinite and I am no-thing.

No matter what — I keep my heart quiet and calm in the tenderness of love. Love is the living breath of my soul. I find joy in the eternal."

That's where "wo-manifestation" begins — in the eternal NOW. Enjoy your *wow of now!* Tell me about your exciting adventures — stay in touch!

"Create the wow of now, a daily legacy. Live and love fully and ecstatically!"

EPILOGUE: The Utopian World According to Wendy Robbins

I recently reviewed the Universal Declaration of Human Rights, President Roosevelt's 2nd Bill of Rights, and a summary Robert Muller's work at the United Nations. I also had a conversation with Karen Paull about the Equal Rights Amendment and how bizarre it is that it hasn't been accepted in the USA since it was first introduced in 1923. This is what it says:

Section 1. Equality of rights under the law shall not be denied or abridged by the United States or by any state on account of sex.

Section 2. The Congress shall have the power to enforce, by appropriate legislation, the provisions of this article.

Section 3. This amendment shall take effect two years after the date of ratification.

That's it. If we change the word "sex" to "gender," would that help it pass? So far, I haven't been able to get an answer from our senators and Congresspeople on what it will take. Maybe you will.

Anyway, I got past my obsession with the Equal Rights Amendment (ERA) and thought about ways to build a utopian global community. I contemplated many plans and developed my own initiatives to create a solid foundation that will radically change the world. It seems that the masses, both conservative and liberal, are aligning themselves with many of these ideas — or at least considering their merits. There is no need to find what you disagree with. Instead, focus on something that inspires, motivates, and activates you to take immediate and consistent action.

I invite you to step up your leadership skills and act on at least one of the ideas you've learned in this book so that you truly create a daily legacy. You make a difference! The stakes have never been higher. The old paradigms and systems don't work, do they? We are now paying the price based on outdated and limited economic, environmental, and worldly beliefs of fear and greed. How is that working for you?

It is time to create a revolution, a worldwide movement with you as the leader. Remember: *if it's to be, it's up to me!* I believe in you — I want to hear about your cause and what you are doing to change the world so we celebrate you and your courage!

Here are some of my ideas:

- The human family prioritizes respect for self and others and accepts responsibility for all actions.
- Love is the foundation of everything. We create a sense of safety and peace by thinking of everyone, even our "enemy," as our "beloved."
- There is no "them." We are all one.
- Heads of countries agree to develop direct, instantaneous contact with one another. This gives the people an important voice to foster peace, settle disputes, and to develop and implement better global solutions to ensure our collective well-being and the future of our planet.

A few ideas to develop are:

- Nuclear-free zones
- Peace zones
- Peace departments that work with the war departments to create alternatives to conflict and genocide
- Worldwide ceasefire for at least a day
- Micro-loans
- Debt forgiveness
- The prioritization of environmental concerns
- The incorporation of elders' and indigenous wisdom to ensure our conscious evolution

- Replacement of ministries of "foreign affairs" with Ministries of Global Cooperation
- Progress that is determined by how people are treated and cared for

Everyone has the right to good education that promotes freedom, tolerance, and a desire for world peace. It will pave the way for the full development and strengthening of respect for human and animal rights, freedom, tolerance, and friendship among all nations, races, and religious groups. Parents have the right to choose the kind of education that their children receive.

People are educated to be entrepreneurs; to question consumption, war, biased media, any type of cruelty to human beings or animals, privatized water rights, and authority. They are free to experience peace and acceptance by learning about all cultures through music, dance, literature, art, science, inventions, and food — all while knowing that different tastes and senses of morality are acceptable as a freedom of expression.

The people of the planet collectively work for, protect, nurture, and take care to ensure that there is clean water and organic food for all — no one goes hungry, as there is currently enough food for everyone. Farmers are subsidized and have the right to raise and sell natural products that sustain the earth and truly nourish people. All political decisions are made to promote fair, healthy, environmental and sustainable well-being for at least seven generations into the future.

All people deserve a comfortable and safe home as well as medical or natural care to maintain and enhance health. All people have the right to start a business offering huge value — based on passion — or to at least get a purposeful job that earns them enough to provide food, clothing, medical benefits, social services, recreation, and the ability to contribute to society.

Everyone is able to save a sufficient amount for retirement. Bartering, volunteering, and selfless service is encouraged. All people deserve paid vacations and fair hours worked in humane conditions. Children will not be used as workers. Sweat shops absolutely will not be tolerated.

All people — without discrimination — have the right to equal pay for equal work. All people have the right to form and join trade unions.

Systems are set up and funded so that elderly, sick, disabled, and unemployed individuals contribute to society in valuable ways so they are not a burden — and they are able to keep their home, eat well, and be educated.

Instead of foreclosing on homes, banks offer owner discounts so people can stay in their homes and pay based on current value and employment. If banks can offer investors foreclosed homes for pennies on the dollar, they can and will offer the same to the owner.

Any company accepting a bailout will not offer huge bonuses to employees or CEOs. They must pay back the loan with interest so the taxpayers make money on it. Any citizen who does not support war will not pay for it and instead can choose to pay taxes toward education or health care.

Businesses will have freedom from unfair competition and domination by monopolies. Greed is not good and is unacceptable. All people will be compensated fairly and equitably based on how much good the companies do for people, animals, and the planet's well-being.

All human beings have the right to life, liberty, and equal protection under the law, with fair and public hearings by an independent and impartial tribunal. Everyone is presumed innocent until proven guilty. All people are given a right to privacy, family, home, or correspondence without attacks upon honor and reputation.

All slavery in any form shall be prohibited, and perpetrators will be punished to the fullest extent of the law. No person shall be subject to discrimination, arbitrary arrest, detention, exile, torture, inhuman or degrading treatment, or punishment. All people deserve dignity, equal rights, freedom, justice, and peace. There will be freedom of speech, belief, thoughts, opinion, expression, religion, worship, truth in media, and peacefully assembly — and freedom from fear.

Our collective global goal is to develop friendly relations between nations where human rights are enjoyed regardless of sex, race, color, age, language, religion, political ideologies, property, or any other status. Marriage is defined as a loving equal-rights relationship between two consenting adults.

Everyone has the right — and is given equal access — to take part in the government, directly or through freely chosen representatives. The will of the people shall be the basis of the authority of government through fair elections, universal and equal suffrage, or fair and balanced voting procedures. Everyone has the right to social security.

If the people lead, the leaders will follow. Of the people, for the people, by the people will be the focus behind every decision governments make.

Mothers and children are entitled to special care and assistance. All children, whether born in or out of wedlock, shall enjoy the same social protection.

The goals are human happiness, a feeling of well-being, freedom to be an individual; and an education promoting peace, sustainability, and tolerance of all people.

ACKNOWLEDGMENTS

First I want to thank my sensational partner, the Leo, Karen Paull, for supporting this seemingly endless process and seeing it be a bestseller when I wrote my first word!

My dogs, Cleopatra and Casanova, kept me understanding what is most important in life — taking long walks while singing funny songs and howling with wild abandon at full amber moons.

Bill Gladstone, who answered my endless questions, presented my book to publishers, and introduced me to Anne Helliker.

To Anne Helliker, the wordsmith who streamlined my ramblings and doesn't suck at grammar like I do, thanks for clever insights and working tirelessly when I was tweaking, freakishly, one word at a time.

Thanks to Danielle Fernandez, who did an amazing job laying out the book and really got that I wanted this to be different from the gazillion other books out there. Talk about patience and a need for excellence — even when we got to version 292, she continued to reply to my revisions with a ;0) in her e-mails. By the way, I found her by outsourcing the job using one of the services I recommended to you.

Kelly Ann Hanrahan — WOW! Thanks for being such a cool ass and for being a model citizen! What a stunning job you did on the book cover and website.

Tom Brennan, thanks for getting word out about the book, ensuring we create a worldwide movement empowering women.

Agnes Fohn, thanks for taking the photo for the book even after we finished shooting a 12-hour day on the TV show.

Thank you, Anita Windisman, for working tirelessly to produce the personalized version of this book! It uses your own name through the book and in the title — so cool! Check it out; it's a great way to experience this book.

Thanks to Hay House and Reid Tracy for choosing to distribute this book around the world! Thanks also to Jill Kramer, Jacqui Clark, Christy Salinas, John Thompson, Jeanne Liberati, and Jami Goddess. And a big thank-you to Richelle Zizian for getting me the media attention so this book becomes a huge bestseller!

Thanks to Roger Cooper and all the top publishers for turning me down so I got to learn everything there is to know about writing, editing, laying out, creating a cover, getting testimonials and ISBN numbers and Library of Congress numbers, creating a website selling the book, getting press and marketing...I wouldn't have gotten a chance to do all this if I wasn't so stubborn. Being told "No" just makes me want to do something even more. Sincerely, thank you!

Thanks to all the amazing mentors who wrote testimonials!

I wrote this book during a hold we had while shooting our TV series, *Homemade Millionaire*. I'm so glad to have used the time to write — I was truly inspired. Our team is amazing! Thanks to everyone for showing me what excellence really is. Kelly Ripa and Mark Consuelos — WOW! Thanks for being my new friends and believing in me against all odds. I'm in deep gratitude. Andrew Strauser, everyone at Milojo, Discovery, TLC. To the HSN/ Home Shopping Network execs — Wahoo! You changed my life by believing in me. Thank you! I love our entire production team. I've never experienced a harder-working and more positive team, ever! Thanks to the inventors for changing their lives in two days. To Ed Evangelista for telling me lame stories, being a great inspiration, and for introducing me to Mark Turner, my theatrical agent at Abrams Agency, who told me it would be great if I were a small person wanting to be 1,000 pounds with 28 kids, since then he could easily sell me.

Thanks everyone for buying The Tingler™ head massager, and to Jorli McLain and her family for the life-changing journey!

Thanks to my family and friends for all the love and support, even when I would disappear for long stretches. Thanks for asking me how the writing process was going when it wasn't really going anywhere. A shout out to Marvin Paull for checking my numbers.

Whew...how lucky am I to have all the cool testimonials from so many mentors and people I respect? I feel so blessed!

Wahoo to Michael Beckwith, Ernest Holmes, and Gurumayi for spiritual nourishment.

Napoleon Hill, thank you for writing *Think and Grow Rich*.

Thanks, Martin Dunkerton and Tianna Conte, for reintroducing me to the book and having me be in your movie.

Randy Garn, what a huge adventure we will take together to change so many lives.

Jamyelese Ryer, thanks for making me godmother to Dakota! I love that his first words were "naked" and "rock and roll" and "freedom!" What more is there to say? :o)

To everyone finding their naked truth, to dancing crazily, to expansive freedom, to embracing your magnificence, the wow of now, overflowing opulence, authentically and lovingly tingling the world!

Thanks to all of you for reading this book, telling your friends, joining our online mastermind network, telling your friends and co-creating a new "ye$ we can" movement. Stop complaining about money — create a revolution! We will change ourselves, thereby changing the world!

ABOUT THE AUTHOR

Wendy Robbins went from being $10,000 in debt to making millions by co-designing and marketing The Tingler™ head massager. She is a leading expert on mastering your millionaire mind-set and bringing your ideas to millions.

She is starring in a TV series with Kelly Ripa *Homemade Millionaire,* which airs on TLC in Fall 2010. On the show, Wendy shows women how to manufacture, market, and pitch their inventions to HSN (Home Shopping Network).

She is also in a movie based on the classic book *Think and Grow Rich.* The film — called *Awaken Your Riches!* — is similar to the best-selling book *The Secret.*

Wendy attended the Juilliard School for acting and directed and produced reality films and TV shows for 13 years. Two films won Emmy's, and she was nominated for a third. She is a member of the Director's Guild, Screen Actor's Guild, and AFTRA. Her art and photography have recently shown in galleries.

She is a popular inspirational speaker who has been onstage in front of thousands, and her testimonials are impressive. She hosted her own radio show for almost three years, reaching more than half a million people, interviewing millionaires and top spiritual leaders.

Wendy co-founded **www.tingletribe.com**, a social network of passionate people committed to making a difference on the planet and to celebrating ordinary people doing extraordinary things. The site offers the resources you need to get your message to millions — and get paid!

She also co-founded **www.tinglenetwork.com**, which reaches 150 million+ people through the Web and mobile apps. If you have a site reaching at least 10,000 unique people a month, with great and unique content, visit the site. If you are a top brand, advertiser, or sponsor, we want to hear from you, too!

To hire Wendy to speak at your event or to get coached by Wendy or one of her elite mentors, go to **www.nowheretomillionaire.com**. There you'll find information on topics, fees, etc. You can also get FREE training, find out about upcoming events, join an online VIP mastermind group, find out about how to get the personalized e-book, get a free sample chapter, get discounts and freebies, and find out about Wendy's inner circle on this site, too!

To access Wendy's media kit, visit **wendy.instantmediakit.com**.